The 100 Stupidest Things Ever Done

Ross and Kathryn Petras

Michael O'Mara Books Limited

First published in Great Britain in 1997 by
Michael O'Mara Books Limited
9 Lion Yard
Tremadoc Road
London SW4 7NQ

First published in America in 1996
by Main Street Books, Doubleday

A CIP catalogue record of this book is available from the British Library

ISBN 1 85479 242 3

Designed by Mick Keates
Typeset by Concise Artisans

Printed in Great Britain by Cox & Wyman Ltd, Reading, Berks

Note: In some cases, the names of individuals have been changed
to protect the innocent, the guilty or the merely foolish.
In all cases, the intention of everything included in this book
has been to amuse – at no one's expense.

Introduction

A few years ago, we put together *The 100 Stupidest Things Ever Said* – a look at the fine art of of placing the foot in the mouth. But we couldn't stop there.

It got us to thinking: what about the *doers* out there? The people of action who, instead of saying something stupid, go right out and *do* something stupid?

It's time to give credit where credit is due.

So now we've collected *The 100 Stupidest Things Ever Done* – a compilation of inane incidents, senseless stunts, farcical feats and utterly asinine activities.

Committing a stupid action isn't as simple as you might think. Actually, it's a bit of a science. As students of stupidity, we've discovered that there are distinct types of stupid action, including:

The Bureaucratic Bungle: when red tape spawns red faces. The inevitable result of following the rules instead of common sense, this type of institutional inanity is committed by any large organisation – from the government to schools to corporations.

The Inspired Idiocy: ingenuity gone insane. This is a stupid action committed by a person with creativity, vision . . . and an amazingly ridiculous idea. Favoured by people who suddenly wonder just why it is that no one has ever crossed the English Channel in a motorised bathtub . . . and who have the nerve (or the insanity) to actually try it.

The Enigmatic Eccentricity: a bit like the inspired idiocy, but more of a lifestyle. This is the speciality of people who make non-conformity into an art form – a dying breed nowadays, as mass culture spawns mass group-think. Happily, there are still enough brave individualistic souls who follow their own drummer, to whatever bizarre and silly ends it may take them.

The Asinine Alibi: when people are caught in the act, but feel it necessary to explain anyway in a futile and ridiculous attempt to clear their name. The result? Looking guilty – and stupid – at the same time. This type of stupidity is especially prevalent in courtrooms, police stations and anywhere politicians are found.

The Big Business Blunder: capitalism run amok. This occurs when business goes overboard in trying to sell a product, make a profit or keep the wheels of commerce turning. It can be something like a global advertising mistranslation that makes people think they can prevent pregnancy by buying certain ink to a product promotion that stinks . . . literally.

The Trying-Too-Hard-Not-to-Make-a-Mistake Mishap: something that happens to everyone at one time or another – especially to anal-retentive perfectionists. You're trying so hard to make everything go well that it all blows up in your face.

The Bad Timing Fiasco: just what it sounds like. Everything is going smoothly, then the worst happens . . . at the worst possible moment. Often occurs just after someone has made a sweeping generalisation like 'this is the safest building ever built' right before the building collapses.

The Preposterous Production: stupidity on stage (or on television or on film). This is a dramatic form of stupidity in action, commonly produced by auteurs who have a unique vision ('King Lear on roller skates!') and wonder why no one else thought of it.

The Politically Correct but Dumb: when people are so worried about being inoffensive that they wind up being idiotic instead. Practised by governments, schools and well-meaning types in particular, this type of stupidity proves that there is such a thing as being too concerned about what other people think.

The Simply Stupid: just plain stupidity, pure and simple.

As an added treat. *The 100 Stupidest Things Ever Done* includes Special Sections on specific areas of stupid actions, such as:

Government Gaffes: a non-partisan, non-ethnocentric, all-inclusive collection of governmental nonsense that proves the public's sneaking suspicion that, if you want something done stupidly, ask the government.

Science Goes Stupid: proof that an advanced degree doesn't necessarily mean you've got the greatest smarts in the world. This section contains examples of the most ridiculous research imaginable.

Idiotic Inventions and Products We Could Live Without: a rundown of utterly useless products that no one needs, but, for some reason, intrepid inventors and not-so-savvy product developers keep foisting on the public.

Stupid Songs: music that doesn't make you want to tap your feet, snap your fingers or sing along, but does make you laugh. This includes lyrics and titles of some of the absolutely worst songs ever written.

Lunatic Laws: a listing of the most ridiculous laws around – evidence that the legal system is as laughable as you might have thought.

Criminally Stupid: examples of extremely *im*-perfect crimes committed by less-than-brilliant criminal minds.

In short, we've made every effort to cover it all. If it's something someone did that's stupid, we've tried to include it. As you can see, *The 100 Stupidest Things Ever Done* is a celebration of all of us – and the stupid things we all do at one time or another. It salutes the buffooneries, travesties of common sense and just plain stupid things people have done.

If you know about – or have committed yourself – something you consider one of the stupidest things ever done, we'd love to hear about it. We're always on the lookout for more stupidities to use in our sequels. Please send us a brief description of the incident and include the date, time and place you heard it or, if it's something you found in the papers or magazines, send us a clipping. And let us know if you want to be credited in print for your contribution. Send your 'stupidest thing ever done' to:

Ross and Kathryn Petras
c/o Michael O'Mara Books Limited
9 Lion Yard
Tremadoc Road
London SW4 7NQ

On Advertising, Great Moments In:

Sumitomo was a giant Japanese steelmaker that developed a special super-tough steel pipe. They were sure it would be snapped up by the Americans.

It was a good product, but there was one problem. Sumitomo had hired a Japanese advertising agency instead of an American one.

The agency named the steel pipe Sumitomo High Toughness, to show up its strength. But to make it all easier to remember, the agency decided to emphasise the initials of the Sumitomo High Toughness steel pipe as a sort of shortened brand name. So, in a series of huge two-page ads in major business magazines throughout the United States, startled customers saw ads like this:

SHT – from Sumitomo
Now, Sumitomo brings SHT to the United States.

At the bottom of the ads, Sumitomo assured customers that their product 'was made to match its name'.

On Age, Importance of, in Hold-ups:

It began as a typical hold-up, this time in Los Angeles in 1994. A young man came into a liquor store, waved his gun at the man behind the counter, and yelled for the clerk to give him all the money in the cash register. And the clerk, realising this wasn't a game, quickly did as he was told.

Then the thief spotted a bottle of good Scotch on the shelf behind the clerk. He asked the clerk to hand that over as well. But this time the clerk didn't comply. 'Absolutely not,' he told the thief.

This wasn't in the usual script. The thief was non-plussed. 'Why can't I have the Scotch?' he asked the clerk.

'You have to be twenty-one to get liquor,' the clerk said – as he probably said hundreds of times a day.

'But I am twenty-one,' protested the thief.

The clerk wouldn't buy it. No legal ID, no booze.

The frustrated thief finally pulled out his wallet and showed his photo driver's licence to the clerk. See, he *was* legal.

Good enough. The clerk gave the bottle to the thief, who left happy.

Then the clerk called the police and gave them the name and address of the thief – who he knew would be charged as an adult.

On Alibis, Hairy:

A burglar, John Bristol, was caught red-handed on his hands and knees in an apartment. But as he told the police, he really wasn't a burglar at all. 'I was passing the time between trains,' he explained.

But what about the screwdriver he was holding?

'I was using it to squash a hairy bug that had attached itself to the front door.'

On Advice, Not Following Your Own:

Mrs. Dwight Morrow was expecting famous financier J. P. Morgan for tea – and she was a bit concerned. The problem was J. P. Morgan's nose. It was large, bright red and altogether conspicuous. Mrs. Morrow was worried that one of her two young daughters, particularly Anne (who later became a writer and married Charles Lindbergh), might say something untoward about Morgan's nose and ruin the tea.

So she sat the two girls down before Morgan was supposed to arrive and explained to them that children sometimes saw odd or interesting things, but they didn't have to comment on them. In particular, she warned them to say nothing at all about any-thing about Mr. Morgan's appearance that might strike them as peculiar.

Mr. Morgan arrived and, much as Mrs. Morrow had feared, little Anne and her sister were transfixed by Morgan's nose. As discreetly as possible, she tried to hurry the girls out of the room before they forgot themselves and said something. Finally the girls curtsied and left the room – and Mrs. Morrow drew her first relaxed breath. The crisis point had passed. They could now have their tea in peace.

'And now, Mr. Morgan,' she said, turning to him, 'will you have one or two lumps of sugar in your nose?'

On Air Travel, Strange:

In early 1983, a man from the Los Angeles area had a great idea: Why not *fly* instead of drive to his girl-friend's house?

The logistics of how he would accomplish this were ingeniously simple. He would get a lightweight pool lounge chair. He would attach helium weather balloons all around the chair. Then he would simply sit in the chair and float upward into the sky. Besides a beer, he would bring with him a small air pistol, to shoot and pop the balloons one by one when he wanted to lose altitude or return to earth.

Simple.

On the day of the flight, things went off without a hitch . . . during the first few minutes. The balloons rose according to plan, carrying the man and his lounge chair up into the sky. As the man achieved his desired altitude, he got ready to shoot a few balloons to stabilise his altitude. He took aim . . . and then dropped the air pistol.

And now the lounge chair kept rising.

At ten thousand feet, the winds took him out near the skies of LAX – Los Angeles International Airport.

The radio tower chatter from airline pilots reported the unusual sight of a man in a lounge chair loafing in the air lanes. One pilot reported a UFO, under the somewhat logical reasoning that he couldn't be seeing a man in a lounge chair with a beer at what was now fifteen thousand feet above the earth . . .

Finally the winds blew the man and lounge chair back towards suburbia. And as the helium slowly leaked out of the balloons, the lounge chair gradually began to descend, and then, fittingly, landed right by the side of a backyard family swimming pool.

On Alibis, Rock Solid:

Christine Powers, the mother of a young man accused of committing a drive-by shooting in New

Orleans, was outraged. The police were clearly trying to frame her son. She was positive he was innocent.

'The facts are black-and-white,' she said. 'Steve couldn't possibly have been involved because, at exactly ten-thirty, when this shooting took place, he was over the other side of town in a housing project, murdering someone who owed us money.'

On Arrests:

Alert police in an English town arrested a man for public drunkenness because of his 'glazed expression'. He was released when he appeared in court and showed the judge his glass eye.

On Anatomy, Extra-Special:

A young man who worked as a fish filleter was a finalist in a British 'Sexy Boy' male beauty contest – and he was definitely making an impression on the judges and the crowd. But just as he left the stage to cheers from those watching, he was asked to step into the inspection tent by a pageant official for closer examination. Something seemed, well, fishy.

The contestant complied. He took off his swim trunks as the official asked. It was then that the official saw why the contestant was such a crowd pleaser: Under the swimsuit, the man was wearing a jockstrap into which a power drill was stuffed. ·

The man claimed that it was all a terrible mistake. He had taken the drill with him for 'security reasons' – 'and just before my name was called, I realised it would be foolish to leave it behind in the dressing room.'

On Ancient Coins, Experts and:

A museum was sponsoring an exhibition of Roman artifacts found nearby. Proudly displayed in one case was a vintage Roman sestertius coin. It was identified by museum experts as having been minted almost two thousand years before, somewhere around A.D. 135.

However, one visiting expert disagreed. Little Fiona Gordon, age nine, identified the coin as a plastic token given away by a local soft drink manufacturer.

Museum experts were amused, and asked her to prove this cute idea. So Fiona pointed out the manufacturer's trademark on the back of the coin.

Embarrassed museum officials started explaining. According to a spokesperson, 'The token was designed as a Roman replica. The trouble was that we construed the letter "R" on the coin to mean "Roma". In fact, it stood for "Robinson's", the soft drink manufacturers.'

The museum promised to view with 'great suspicion' any coins donated in the future.

B

On Bee Avoidance Moves:

A man was fishing in the Amazon's Rio Negro when his line got stuck in a tree. He began pulling and tugging at the line to free it, when the line hit a bees' nest. The infuriated bees went for him. He swatted, jumped, ran, but the bees kept attacking. Desperate to get away, he finally leaped into the river.

He was promptly eaten by piranhas.

On Bank Robbers, Far-sighted:

It was a lot like a scene from a gangster movie: two masked men rushed into a bank (it happened to be in Jaumpur in the Indian state of Uttar Pradesh), guns drawn and demanded that the manager behind the counter hand over the money – pronto.

Although the guns were very convincing, the manager hesitated. He didn't have any money, he explained.

'Impossible. Isn't this a bank?' one of the robbers asked.

'Yes. An eye bank.'

There is a happy ending, though. The manager wound up convincing the robbers to pledge their eyes.

On Bank Robbers, Revolving:

Three men decided to rob the Royal Bank of Scotland in 1975. But they got off on the wrong foot – and never recovered.

It all started when they got stuck in the revolving doors of the bank entrance. The incompetent criminals were finally freed by the bank staff, and they left the building.

They reappeared a few minutes later and announced they were robbing the bank. But the reaction wasn't what they expected. Everyone burst into laughter. Everyone thought it was a wonderful practical joke.

The robbers persisted. First they asked for £5,000 but the cashier was laughing so hard that he didn't give it to them. The desperate robbers reduced their demand to £500, then £50. Finally they asked for anything, just *anything*. But to no avail.

Finally, in desperation, one of the trio vaulted

over the counter to get the money. But instead he tripped and landed on his ankle, badly spraining it. The other two now decided to make their getaway. They got as far as the revolving door... where they got stuck again.

On Blackmail, Bad Set-ups:

A man with a beautiful girlfriend had a perfect plan for raising cash. He would find a rich married lawyer, she would seduce him, and together they would blackmail the sucker!

It couldn't fail.

So, one night, while his girlfriend accomplice attracted the right rich lawyer, the man hid in her hotel room closet with a flash camera ready.

Soon the girlfriend brought the lawyer into the room and, not long afterwards, love-making began.

Steady, now! The man waited for just the right moment. Then – *snap!* – the picture was taken and the man triumphantly burst open the closet and demanded blackmail money from the lawyer.

All seemed fine until the lawyer looked at the picture – it was a wonderful shot of the refrigerator in the corner of the room.

On Bookshops:

Whenever anyone says that literacy isn't declining, consider this story from a woman who recently went to a bookshop to find a copy of *Mein Kampf*.

The bookseller asked: 'Is that the author?'

The woman answered: 'No, it's German for *My Struggle*. It's by Hitler.'

The bookseller: 'Hitler who?'

The woman: 'Are you serious?'

The bookseller (raising eyes in pained look): 'Look. I don't know *every* author in the world.'

On Bullfights:

Spain has always loved bullfights.

But when the country was under the rule of Generalissimo Francisco Franco, it was decided that sticking and killing bulls just wasn't brutal enough.

So they decided to enliven things a bit. They took a bull and, for an added touch, put a tiger into the ring.

The fascist crowd at the bullfight went wild with excitement. A *bull and tiger* fight!

But the tiger was a gentle sort. Instead of ripping the bull apart, he sat down in the middle of the ring, next to the bull, and started licking it.

This love fest continued for some time. The crowd got angrier and angrier. Soon furious fascists were booing, then more lively ones began throwing things at the happy couple. Finally a mob jumped into the ring and started kicking the lackadaisical bull and tiger. The bull and tiger didn't like this and started getting aggressive – against the crowd.

And that's when General Franco's elite fascist military police decided to take things in hand. Firing machine guns, they entered the ring. They somehow missed the tiger and only wounded the bull, but they did manage to machine-gun and kill seventeen overexcited spectators.

On Burglary Methods, Indiscreet:

The key to burglary is to pick your target well.

This was where a burglar in Longmont, Colorado, went wrong. All was going well at the store he was attempting to rob. He was busy prying open the front door with a crowbar. Then he stopped. Something seemed a little wrong . . .

He looked up. A large number of people were inside the store. And they were staring at him.

At this moment, the master burglar realised that the store was still open.

On Bureaucracy, Great Moments in, Elevator:

Q: Why did the three New Jersey towns of Upper Pittsgrove, Alloway and Quinton each hire an elevator inspector when there were absolutely no elevators in any building in any of the towns?
A: Because the state government told them to.

With impeccable bureaucratic logic, the New Jersey Department of Consumer Affairs explained that by law all 567 towns in New Jersey are required to have elevator inspectors.

Even if the town doesn't have an elevator?

No exceptions, a brilliant bureaucratic spokesperson explained. 'Otherwise, the Uniform Construction Code would no longer be uniform.'

On Concerts, Explosive:

The new conductor of the Atlanta Symphony back in 1974 wanted to celebrate his appointment by adding a little zip to the performance of the *1812 Overture*.

So he put sixteen mini cannons throughout the auditorium. They were to be fired electronically, one by one, during the middle and the climatic end of the overture.

As the orchestra reached the middle of the overture, the conductor pressed the button for cannon number one.

Unfortunately, it didn't work out as planned. With a roar, all sixteen cannons fired at the same time. The audience of fifteen thousand was stunned. The booming of the cannons was followed by billows of cannon smoke filling the room, choking many in the audience. But it wasn't over yet. Now the wonderful Smell-All-Tell-All Customer Safety System started sounding and spraying, drenching everyone in special antiburn foam. Despite the smoke and foam, some dazed audience members managed to make it to what they thought was safety in the foyer – only to be trampled by charging fire-men with masks shouting 'Geronimo!' as they rushed inside.

'I have to admit to a number of incidents,' said the fire chief. 'The fighters were wearing a new model of smoke mask and some of them could not see.'

On Campaign Advertising:

It was election time in Ecuador. And a company that put out a foot deodorant called Pulvapies decided to tie in their advertising campaign with the upcoming municipal elections. They came up with a clever slogan: 'Vote for any candidate, but if you want well-being and hygiene, vote for Pulvapies.'

Then came phase two of the ad campaign, an equally ingenious tie-in: on election eve, the company rolled out nationwide distribution of a leaflet designed to look just like a ballot. The leaflet read: FOR MAYOR: HONOURABLE PULVAPIES.

The campaign was effective – but not in the way the company had planned. Yes, Pulvapies increased sales. It also got votes across the country, as befuddled voters marked their ballots for the Honourable Pulvapies – and, by a definitive majority, the footpowder was elected mayor of the small coastal town of Picoaza.

On Campaigns, Stupid Moments in:

Dan Quayle, extending his hand during a campaign stop at Hardee's: 'I'm Dan Quayle. Who are you?' Woman: 'I'm your Secret Service agent.'

On Car Testing, Stupid Moves in:

LaVerie Williams of Beaumont, Texas, was thrilled with her new car and wanted to test every aspect of it – including the capacity of the car's trunk. So she had family members shut her inside the trunk.

That's when she realised she had the keys clutched in her hand.

On Character Assessment:

The parishioners of a Baptist church in Illinois didn't know what they were getting when Charles Lewis first became a pastor. All they did know was that he had what is politely called 'a bad past'.

But during his first address to the people of the church, he decided it was the right moment to make a completely clean breast of it. From the pulpit, he revealed the horrible truth about his past: he was a reformed Mafia hit man who had killed twenty-eight people over fifteen years while working for Murder Incorporated – but while on Death Row, he found God and became reformed. That wasn't all, though. Even after his reformation, he wasn't completely clean. He had been one of the committee that planned the entire Watergate conspiracy.

The church leaders and worshippers were impressed by his willingness to be completely frank. They decided to let bygones be bygones.

But then the church got a shock about Pastor Lewis: none of his confessed sins had ever taken place.

'When the local police revealed that these incidents had never taken place – although he had strangled his second wife in 1987,' said church leader Dr. Donald Morley, 'we decided that he was not the man we thought he was.'

On Contests, Decisive:

The question of who owned a certain sago palm tree in Haruku, Indonesia, was the cause of a dispute between two men, a certain Mr. Djambi and a Mr. Hasnuddin.

Rather than fight or go to court, they decided to go back to traditional Indonesian ways and have a little contest. The winner would get the palm tree.

The contest rules were simple: whoever could hold his breath underwater the longest would win. Watched by their fellow villagers, Mr. Djambi and Mr. Hasnuddin weighted themselves down with stones, took two deep breaths, jumped into the water, and then held their breaths.

Unfortunately, it was a tie . . . they both drowned.

On Carmen, Uncommon Production of:

Opera fans in Heidelberg, Germany, were watching a first-class production of the opera *Carmen*, conducted by Ian Reid. At last, the moment the audience had been waiting for – the climactic scene when Don José stabs Carmen in the heart with his knife.

Unfortunately, when the actor playing Don José approached Carmen for the fatal stab, he realised something horrible. He had forgotten his toy knife! Still singing away lustily, Don José thought quickly. He would pretend to strangle Carmen instead.

He proceeded to put his hands around Carmen's neck. But the woman playing Carmen didn't know Don José had forgotten his toy knife . . .

She thought he had gone insane. She fought back fiercely, struggling to break herself free. It made for exciting theatre. And in theatre's best traditions, even as she thought her end was near, the woman playing Carmen kept right on singing – although the critics all agreed that her voice was a bit muffled.

On Cleaning Elevators, Ups and Downs in:

A janitor at a Marriott Hotel in England, was asked to clean an elevator. The job took him four full days.

His confused supervisor asked him why it had taken so long. Replied the janitor, 'Well, there are twelve of them, one on each floor, and sometimes some of them aren't there.'

Apparently, the man thought that each floor had a different elevator – so he went to each floor and cleaned the same elevator twelve separate times.

On Composers, Deadbeat:

The Hong Kong tax authorities are tough. They're always on the prowl for tax evaders, particularly foreign singers and entertainers who give performances and then skip off without paying tax.

In 1984, the Hong Kong Philharmonic Society received a strongly worded letter from these tough tax men. The letter came right to the point: there was no report of tax payment from an individual who they knew was connected to the Philharmonic.

The person in question was a certain J. S. Bach, who, according to their records, had recently put on one of his concerts.

On Counterfeiting:

A convenience store clerk in Abilene, Texas, was passed a counterfeit $100 bill – and accepted it without question . . . even though it was a foot long and five inches wide.

On Crime Hauls, the Bottom Line:

Mark Mueller was possibly one of the only thieves to beg the officer who arrested him to book him on manslaughter charges instead of theft.

It all happened when the sensitive thief was

caught red-handed outside of the Globe Freezer Company offices in Colorado. A special investigator spotted him and asked to see the bag he was carrying.

The investigator looked inside the bag and started laughing. When he stopped, he said, 'Do you know what's in here?'

Mueller first said he wasn't sure about the meaning of the word 'here'.

Then the officer told him what was inside the plastic sack he had stolen: 1,800 beef rectums.

'When I told him the sack contained beef assholes,' the investigator told the *Rocky Mountain News*, 'he burst into tears and asked me to book him on a manslaughter charge. Otherwise, he said, he would be the butt of cruel jokes while in prison.'

On Crowd-Pleasing Exposures, Boxers and:

Featherweight boxer Richard Procter was raring to go. He jumped into the ring at the World Sporting Club in London, threw his robe in the corner, and raised his gloves in the air.

He was thrilled at the incredible reception he got from the crowd – wild cheers, whistles, applause.

It was then that he realised he had forgotten to put his shorts on.

On Crime Prevention:

A Western businessman living in Japan had been warned about notorious pickpockets in the Tokyo subways. These notorious thieves operated during the crowded rush hour. They had a habit of grabbing wallets just as subway doors were closing, leaving the victim stuck on the train while they made off with the loot.

One morning the Western businessman was at his usual subway stop when the train pulled in. He boarded, and sure enough, just as the train doors were about to close, he felt a man rub against him.

In a panic, the Western businessman reached for his wallet. It was gone! He looked up as the doors began to close and saw that the man who had rubbed against him had now stepped off the train. And the man was looking at him with what can only be described as a victorious sneer.

Thinking fast, the businessman reached his hands between the closing train doors and grabbed the sneering thief's suit lapels. The doors closed, with the thief still on the platform, but with his lapels trapped between the doors in the tight grip of the businessman.

And now, as the train began to pull away, the expression on the thief's face changed. He began screaming as he ran along the platform with the train. Finally, halfway along the platform, the panicky thief grabbed a stanchion and his lapels tore away.

As the train entered the tunnel, the businessman thought that at least he had gotten something back for his loss.

When he reached his office, he called his wife to get his credit card numbers so he could cancel them. 'But, honey,' she said, 'I've been waiting to call you. You left your wallet on the dressing table when you went to work today.'

On Customers, Surefire Ways to Attract:

It was a fact: the Heavenly Moon restaurant in Beijing, China, served bad food.

According to the public health officer, the squid with oyster sauce 'was the worst I have eaten in thirty-seven years of public service'. Other customers thought the same thing – the meat was tough, the oils were rancid, the food was greasy. Which is what made the restaurant's popularity so odd . . . .

As one customer noted, 'I always left the Heavenly Moon telling them their food tasted like dog dirt. Yet somehow I always went back the next day.' A lot of other people were doing the same thing. In spite of the horrible food, on most days, long lines formed outside the Heavenly Moon hours before it opened.

Just what was the Heavenly Moon's secret?

Public health investigators began looking into this. They learned that the restaurant had started getting popular a few months back, after someone had thrown a dinner out the window in anger at its absolute awfulness. Apparently, the owner had retired to the kitchen for some thinking. The sauce! That was it. He would spice up the food by adding a special seasoning sauce to all the dishes!

And it worked. Most customers found the sauce a bit greasy, but they all found it strangely compelling....

The lines got longer and longer. Even the investigators themselves started frequenting the restaurant, using their influence to book space weeks ahead.

When police finally moved in, they discovered the special sauce indeed had one very compelling ingredient. Pure opium paste.

In his defence, the restaurateur said, 'They do it in all the restaurants in America.'

SPECIAL SECTION
Criminally Stupid:

'Crime does not pay.' This used to be the message in every film and every comic book in the land. Times have changed, of course, and nowadays crime often does pay, as any half-second watching the TV news can tell you.

So maybe that's why this collection of criminally stupid capers is so refreshing, so recherché. It harkens back to a simpler time, when the criminal always got caught. And it warms the cockles of the heart of any scared suburbanite with a new alarm system and triple locks – a lot of criminals out there are truly, wonderfully incompetent. Maybe there isn't so much to be afraid of, after all.

☞ A burglar had finished robbing an apartment in Connecticut and decided that, instead of lugging his loot home on foot, he'd have a cab pick him up. So he called a taxi. It didn't come in the promised time, so he called again. Still no cab. He called twice more – but the police, alerted of an intruder in the apartment by a neighbour, came before the cab arrived. The burglar's only comment? 'I'm never going to use that company again,' he complained.

☞ A Detroit bank robber passed a note to a bank teller – and it said the standard thing: he was armed and the teller was to fill a bag with cash.

But then the robber broke from tradition. Noticing all the video surveillance cameras around the bank and hesitant to be photographed too much, he told the teller he'd wait outside for the cash. 'Just bring it out when you've got it ready.' He went outside – and the police, called by the teller the second he left, caught him there, patiently waiting.

☞ A Jacksonville, Florida, robber couldn't quite get it together when it came to disguising himself. He stuck up a grocery store, wearing a paper bag with cut-out eyeholes over his head. But during the attempted stickup, the bag shifted and the eyeholes were no longer over his eyes, so he couldn't see a thing. To make matters worse, a few seconds later the bag split open, completely revealing his face to the sales clerk. She immediately recognised him as a regular customer – and called the cops when he left.

☞ It looked like a typical bank robbery: two men ran into a Los Angeles bank, brandishing shotguns. 'Everyone lie down on the floor!' yelled one of them. His tone – and the shotguns – convinced everyone that they had better do what he said. And that's what everyone did – tellers, security guards, customers all immediately fell to the floor. In fact, everyone was so obedient that there was no one left standing to get the robbers the money. The two robbers stood there confused for a second, then ran away.

☞ In 1978, a Danish bank robber ran out of the bank he had just robbed, clutching the money. He had no getaway car waiting, but had counted on finding a cab on the busy street. And he wasn't disappointed. He immediately saw a car with a light on the roof, flagged it down, and leaped into the back seat, shouting out his address and telling the driver to step on it. But in his haste, he didn't realise one thing: it wasn't a cab he flagged down, but a police car.

☞ Frank Gort, a San Antonio burglar, was caught and convicted. When it came time for sentencing, the judge gave him seven years. Gort was very upset – and begged the judge not to sentence him to seven years because seven was his unlucky number. The understanding judge complied. He gave him eight years.

☞ An accused bag snatcher was on trial in Tulsa, Oklahoma. Instead of going with the court-appointed defence lawyer, the thief decided he could defend himself better. So, even though he had no legal experience, he served as his own counsel. And everything went beautifully. He presented his case, seemed calm, cool and collected – even during his cross-examination of the woman whose bag he was accused of taking – and was beginning to think he'd get off. Finally he zeroed in for his final question: 'Did you get a good look at my face when I took your bag?' He got ten years.

☞ A man named George Walsh of Blandford, Dorset, was arrested and charged with drunken driving. When he was asked for his name (and identification to back it up), he had a little explaining to do. On his driver's licence, he was listed as Welsh. On his insurance, as Wilsh. On his automobile club membership, as Wulsh. And on an envelope he happened to have in his pocket, as Wlesh. All this because, he said, he was wanted by the IRA and so wanted to disguise his identity. He was ultimately charged under his *real* name: Fred Miller.

☞ A man from Texas City, Texas, was dragging a newspaper vending machine toward his still-running vehicle when he was spotted by the police. As the police officers got near, the man stopped and began reading the paper inside. He explained to the police officers that he had dragged the machine over so he could read the paper better. When one of the officers pointed out that the light was brighter where the vending machine had originally been, the man said, 'I read better in the dark.'

☞ Two Michigan robbers charged into a Detroit music store, waving their guns. 'Nobody move!' one of the robbers ordered. The second robber then moved – and the first shot him in the head.

On Demolitions, Dumb:

In Pompano Beach, Florida, a retired security guard and her husband were having their usual quiet day. They had just begun to eat a light snack in front of the TV, when suddenly they heard loud noises out-side – and then their house began to shake.

Someone was demolishing their house.

They leaped up. The husband tried to open the front door, but found it completely blocked by a bulldozer. His wife was luckier – she managed to get out a side window. Once outside, she confronted the man in charge, the assistant building director, and asked him what was going on. He replied by asking what had happened to the demolition order his department had sent them three months before.

Before she had a chance to tell him there had been some mistake, the bulldozer had ploughed through the side of the house.

At this point, the husband ran outside and con-fronted the building department official. Finally the official realised there had been a bit of a slip-up and stopped his demolition crew.

'Okay, it's a bit messy,' he breezily said. 'But since

we've only removed one load-bearing wall, you don't have that much to complain about. A coat of paint and it will be as good as new.'

As the woman later said to a newspaper reporter, 'It was then that we attacked him.'

On Debates, Great Moments in:

The Oxford debating society is known for its erudite debaters and its high level of scholarship. So when English historian Philip Guedalla was the young president of the Oxford debating society, he was very eager to show what a hot debater he was.

Guedalla came up with a great way of sounding particularly bright and witty. Before a debate, there were open questions from the audience. He asked a friend to ask him two specific questions, for which he had prepared sharp answers. The friend agreed.

The night of the debate the friend in the audience asked the first question. Guedalla came back with his witty and learned reply. The audience howled with laughter. He was just *so* witty!

Guedalla's answer to the second question was even more brilliant. The entire audience broke into spontaneous applause. Guedalla was ecstatic. This little trick was earning him a big reputation! When the applause ended, the friend stood up once more.

'What was the third question you wanted me to ask you?'

On Driving Tests:

In West London, a man was taking a driving test to get his licence to drive his motor scooter. At the test centre, he was given the instructions they always gave out: he was supposed to drive on a specific route. To determine his driving skill, he would be observed by a hidden examiner. And, at some point during the drive, this examiner would suddenly appear and step in front of the scooter. This would test his braking reaction.

Easy enough. The man dutifully followed the instructions, driving carefully through the route. But when he reached the end of it, the examiner hadn't appeared in front of the scooter. So the man drove through the route another time. Then another. Still no examiner.

Finally the man pulled up to the test centre and asked what was going on. He had driven through the route three times and hadn't seen the examiner. Where was he?

'We're sorry,' he was told. 'He stepped in front of the wrong scooter.'

On Defence, Honesty in:

An Oklahoma man was charged with armed robbery of a store – and decided to represent himself in court. All went smoothly, until the store manager took the stand.

'Can you identify the man who held up your store?' she was asked.

'Yes. That's him,' she said, pointing to the defendant. The defendant leaped to his feet and accused her of lying. 'I should have blown your f***ing head off!' he shouted. A quick pause, then he added, 'If I'd been the one that was there.'

On Defendants, Overly Helpful:

Two men were on trial in San Diego, accused of armed robbery. An eyewitness was on the stand being questioned by the prosecutor, who was taking the witness step-by-step through the incident.

'Were you at the scene when the robbery took place?' asked the prosecutor.

'Yes.'

'Did you see a vehicle leave in a rush?'

Again the witness replied yes.

'Did you observe the occupants of the vehicle?'

'Yes. There were two men in the car.'

Perfect. The prosecutor moved in for the kill. 'Are those two men present in court today?'

At that, the two defendants helpfully raised their hands.

On Diplomacy, Great Moments in:

As Luxembourg is such a tiny country, it was decided that it didn't need to attend the European Security Conference in Helsinki. Instead, it asked the Dutch representative to look after its interests.

The Dutch representative took the job of representing both countries conscientiously, maybe a little too conscientiously. . . .

When the debate over how the conference was going to be paid for began, the Dutch diplomat ran around the conference table to the place marked LUXEMBOURG and said, in French, that the United Nations should pay.

Then the Dutch diplomat got back up and ran quickly over to the seat marked NETHERLANDS and said, in English, that each nation should pay separately.

E

On Elections, Sneaky:

The race for city judge in Anderson, Indiana, deserves mention for either extreme stupidity – or amazing creativity – on the parts of those running.

City Judge Donald R. Phillippe was up for re-election and was running against two opponents in the Democratic primary. Polls indicated that Phillippe was way ahead, due to name recognition. So his two opponents filed petitions to change their names.

Opponent number one wanted to change his name to Donald R. Phillippe; opponent number two to ... Donald R. Phillippe.

On Elvis is Alive, Proof of:

There's always someone somewhere who claims to have had an Elvis sighting. Most people who claim to have seen Elvis still alive wind up calling the *National Enquirer*. Sometimes the people at the

Enquirer follow up, but often they don't. However, this particular time they were definitely intrigued.

It wasn't the usual type of Elvis spotter, but a retired Harvard professor. And he said he had 'irrefutable photographic evidence' that Elvis was actually alive.

So the *Enquirer* sent a reporter to the professor's remote home in the mountains of northern Vermont. When the reporter arrived, the elderly professor took him downstairs to the basement, where the professor unlocked the door to the room where he kept the evidence. Then finally the reporter was able to see it himself. It was one snapshot, a shot of the professor standing in front of the house – alone.

The reporter didn't get it. 'Where's the photographic proof of Elvis?' he asked the professor.

'Well,' replied the professor, 'Elvis took the photo.'

On Environmental Scientists:

Scientists were puzzled. According to their state-of-the-art air pollution monitoring equipment worth hundreds of thousands of pounds, Newcastle was by far the most polluted city in England – if not the world. It was so polluted that the readings were literally off the charts. For two years the scientists pondered: why was this city's air so fantastically polluted? What could be causing this phenomenon?

It took a little time, but finally the answer became clear: the super air pollution monitoring machine had been placed right over a lorry parking lot.

On English Channel Crossings:

In the late 1960s, Kenneth Blyton managed to successfully cross the English Channel in a metal bottle driven by a small motor. It was his third crossing, but his first time by bottle. When he landed at Cap Gris Nez, he laid out his next plan of attack.

'I have already crossed by bedstead and by barrel,' he said. 'Next year I intend to cross by giant banana.'

On Escapes, Not-So-Great:

Charles Haggard decided to rob one of those giant do-it-yourself home shopping centres.

But alert police caught him in the act and started to chase him. As Haggard ran, he saw a door. He opened it and ran through. Then he saw another door, which he opened and ran through, then another door...

In all, Haggard ran through eleven fake doors before running into a brick wall and knocking himself out.

On Excuses, Criminally Weak:

A criminal was arrested for burglary and breaking and entering. But he explained that it was all actually a mistake. 'I felt tired,' he said, 'so I rested my head against the shop window and it fell in.'

But what about police who saw him wearing a fur coat from the store? 'I wore it to keep the dust off my sports coat.'

And what about witnesses who saw him trying to knock a hole in the ceiling of the building? 'I could not think of anything else to do at the time.'

On Exposure, Stupid:

'I am not scum,' declared Jagdish Desai to the court in Singapore. 'I admit I dropped my pants in front of this woman...but fate was to blame.'

Jagdish's excuse for indecent exposure was a first in judicial history. It turns out he was walking near the subway station when he spied a mango tree. And then, as he put it: 'I was hungry, so naturally I climbed [the tree] to pick some mangoes.'

Naturally. But then Jagdish accidentally disturbed an ants' nest. And this is where his problems began.

As Jagdish explained: 'When I got down, the ants began biting my private parts, so I went into the subway, took all my clothes off, and rubbed myself to brush them away. Any sane man would have done the same. Unfortunately, this woman happened by, completely misunderstood my intentions, and panicked. I invited her to come closer to see the ants for herself, but she only screamed and reported me to the station master, who had me arrested.'

The judge evidently agreed. Desai's case was dismissed – 'as long as accidental exposures don't occur again'.

On Explanations, Too Precise:

There's a time to be specific and a time to keep your mouth shut. Barry Shoemaker of Harlingen, Texas learned it the hard way. He wound up being arrested because he was painstakingly specific.

To be more precise: Shoemaker was at a meeting of the Harlingen city commission, watching the proceedings and enjoying a smoke. The city manager noticed him in the audience and explained that no cigarette smoking was allowed. Would he please put it out?

Shoemaker got technical. 'It's not a cigarette,' he explained. 'It's a joint.'

On Explorers, Bad:

A man from Olive, Kentucky had a dream. A dream that would take him away from the rolling hills of the Bluegrass State. The dream: to row across the icy Bering Strait, between Alaska and Russia, in a bathtub.

Unfortunately, the dream was not completely fulfilled. According to the explorer, 'I took four gallons of peanut butter along, but on the morning of the fourth day it had gone solid. By late afternoon, although the sun was still high, the sea went rather thick. Next morning I was frozen in.'

No problem. He abandoned the bathtub and walked to land.

f

On Filmstrips, Brazilian-Style:

Back in November 1974, the famous movie *The Exorcist* came to La Pampa Cinema in Rio de Janeiro. But the audience soon was distracted by more than the devil possessing a little girl.

First, a rat began scampering about back and forth next to the screen stage, distracting viewers. The distraction got worse when an usherette, armed with a mop, began chasing the rat in front of the screen.

The angry crowd began yelling, 'Take them off,' meaning, of course, that the theatre management should take the usherette, the mop, and the rat off the stage. But the usherette didn't get the gist of the audience's words. She took them...more literally. After hitting the rat with the mop, she proceeded to take all her clothes off, and then, searching for something else to do, she started dancing nude in the projector light.

She stopped after the police arrived. As she explained to them, 'I thought the audience was calling for me. I was as surprised as anyone.'

On Flotation Devices, Dangers of:

It was another day at the seashore, when a dramatic sea rescue had to take place.

A little girl floated too far offshore on a pair of plastic inflatable teeth. She was rescued by a man – floating on an inflatable lobster.

Said a Coast Guard officer: 'This sort of thing is all too common.'

On Following Instructions, Literal Moments:

A young man named Will Smith was in line at Detroit's busy licence bureau, patiently waiting for his turn to apply for a driver's licence. Finally he reached the desk. The clerk shoved an application across to Smith and brusquely asked him to write his last name first and first name last.

Smith looked confused. 'How's that again?'

'Like I said,' the harried clerk said. 'Write your name backward.'

Good enough. Smith shrugged and followed orders, slowly writing 'lliW htimS'.

G

On Gas Siphoning:

Siphoning gasoline out of a tank isn't exactly a job for the weak-stomached. Often a person doing it sticks a siphoning tube into a tank and begins siphoning out the contents with his mouth. It's not pleasant, but it's doable.

And this is what a thief intended to do in New Zealand in the spring of 1994.

An elderly couple at an East Coast campsite were awakened by sounds outside their mobile home. Too frightened to investigate what was going on, they stayed indoors, listening to the noises outside and waiting for morning. They went outside in the morning and realised that their fears had been well-founded. Outside of their mobile home, they found a siphoning hose, a gasoline can and a metal cap from one of the tanks on the vehicle. Clearly, the thief had intended to siphon gasoline from the mobile home while its occupants were asleep. But the pool of vomit on the ground by the cap proved that something had gone wrong.

Putting the pieces together, they realised just what had happened: the man had removed the cap from a tank, stuck the tube in, and started siphoning. But he had made a crucial error.

He had removed the cap from the sewage holding tank.

On the Geraldo Show, Stupid Breathtaking Moments from:

Miami Vice was still one of the hottest shows on television. And Geraldo Rivera decided to do a news show revealing the *real* side of drug trafficking in the United States: 'American Vice: The Doping of a Nation'.

To make it even more dramatic and immediate, Rivera included a live segment showing a drug raid on a duplex. In this house, Rivera said on-air as viewers watched the cops ready to break in, 'an alleged pimp and prostitute – a dude and his lady – real pros – are supplying truckers speed.'

The cops burst into the house, followed closely by the camera crew, catching the entire dramatic incident live.

A woman, all alone, wearing a shirt and shorts, was painting the walls.

On Getaways:

It should have been a basic armed robbery. Two men from Edmonton, Canada, pulled into the Petro-Canada gas station in Vancouver, Canada, pulled their guns, locked the terrified attendant in the bathroom, and made off with $100. It was a clean getaway.

But twenty minutes later, the not-so-dynamic duo realised they were lost. Finally they decided to risk it and ask for directions, so they pulled into a gas station.

Somehow they didn't realise that they were at the same station they had robbed earlier – and the cashier they asked directions from was the man they had locked in the bathroom before. He played it cool, gave them directions, and, as soon as they started walking away again, he began calling the police.

Then the robbers returned yet another time.

This time their car wouldn't start – and they needed a mechanic. When they learned that there was no mechanic on until eight the following morning, they kept trying to start the car themselves.

The police finally arrived and the crooks were still there. This time they were on the phone, trying to call a tow truck.

Their battery had finally given out.

On Getaways, Failed:

After robbing a tavern in New Athens, Illinois at gunpoint, the robber ran outside to his getaway car. But in the excitement of the robbery, he had lost his keys. What to do?

Better thieves might run – but this man had an even better idea. He stripped off his clothes to his underwear and went back inside the tavern, saying he had been robbed, too.

Unfortunately, despite a dismal attempt at disguising his voice, absolutely everyone in the tavern recognised him. He was arrested.

On Getting the Vote Out, Over-zealous Attempts at:

Herbert Connolly wanted to keep his seat on the Massachusetts Governor's Council badly... *very* badly.

So he did what many candidates do: he campaigned vigorously right to the last minute. He raced around, making speeches, shaking hands and urging people to rush to the polls and vote.

He was so busy doing all this that, by the time he got to the voting booth himself, it had been closed for fifteen minutes.

The good news was that all that extra campaigning netted him 14,715 votes. The bad news was that his opponent got 14,716.

On Getting Too Close to the Story, the Media:

On 9 June 1978, Mr. Bob Specas was ready to beat a domino record by knocking down 100,000 dominoes in a row.

The media was there to broadcast the historic event. A TV camera recorded his progress as Specas set up the last dominoes for his performance.

97,497...97,498...97,499. Then a TV cameraman dropped his press badge... and the dominoes went off.

On Golf, Need for a Hard Head When Playing:

It was the final round of the 1934 U.S. Open and the pressure was on. Bobby Cruickshank was two strokes ahead of his competitors. He had to make he next hole in four strokes to keep his lead.

Cruickshank's drive off the tee was fine. But his

following approach shot was too weak. With horror, he watched the ball sink with a splash into the stream in front of the green – and his heart sank along with it.

A split second later, the ball bounced back out of the water – apparently ricocheting off a sub-merged rock – and rolled onto the green only feet from the hole.

It was a miracle. With a whoop, Cruickshank tossed his club in the air, tipped his hat, and yelled to the heavens, 'Thank you, God!'

That's when Cruickshank got his second shock of the day.

The club, so cheerfully tossed into the air, began hurtling earthward. It came down hard, cracked him on the head, and knocked him to the ground.

He managed to get up again, but he couldn't regain his steadiness. After his great start, he wound up finishing third.

SPECIAL SECTION

Government Gaffes:

I don't make jokes. I just watch the government and report the facts. – Will Rogers

No one said it better than Will Rogers back in the 1930s. Humorists searching for material have little more to do than go to Washington or to their nearest town hall meeting to see stupidity in action.

Of course, we the people foot the bill for all this. And that's why, in order for you to get your money's worth out of your taxes we've included this section.

The government may no longer keep the streets safe, the rubbish collected, or your family healthy. But they can still dish out the laughs.

☞ Governor William Donald Schaefer of Maryland decided to raise the morale of his state, so he appointed a task force on self-esteem. After eighteen months of study, the task force reported that it had identified exactly 1,050 things that Maryland residents were doing to make each other feel better about themselves. Unfortunately, the task force also concluded that it didn't have the money to let any Maryland residents know just what these 1,050 things were.

☞ The Indiana State Police instituted an intensive three-month investigation into the suspicious death of one man. Their findings after their in-depth investigation: the man, who had died of thirty-two hammer blows to the head, was not a suicide but the victim of a murder.

☞ A post office in Ohio discovered that they hadn't done their bit to spread holiday good cheer. About twelve thousand letters were stamped with YOU BITCH instead of MERRY CHRISTMAS before the error was discovered.

☞ The Pennsylvania state government introduced a bill in late 1994 to take care of a pressing matter – that of people 'libelling' fruits, vegetables and seafood. Under the proposed bill, growers, manufacturers and marketers of perishable food could 'attempt to recover damages for the disparagement of any such food product or commodity'.

☞ In 1978, State Representative John Galbraith of Ohio came up with a novel idea for reducing energy usage: he introduced a bill to abolish January and February. His reasoning: 'If we divided the fifty-nine extra days between July and August, we will cut our energy needs by about one-third through eliminating the coldest days of the year. Cold is largely a psychological matter. If people look at the calendar and see that it is July, they will be quite happy to turn the heat down.'

☞ The Wildlife Division of Ohio spent over $25,000 in wages tracking down a notorious criminal. A team of fourteen agents and two undercover agents spent three weeks on the job –

keeping surveillance, taking photographs from nearby bushes, even buying products undercover from the criminal...who happened to be an eight-year-old boy who had committed the heinous act of selling illegal bait. The boy had a stand outside his parents' house from which he sold worms to passing fishermen. It turned out that, aside from the two undercover agents, he had sold bait to only four fishermen. The case was dismissed – but it had cost Ohio enough money to buy twenty-seven tons of worms.

☞ In 1990, the Houston city council wanted to draft an ordinance to outlaw bare women's breasts. To make sure the language was just so, they hired a researcher. His task – to detail why women's breasts are different from men's.

☞ In the late 1980s, New York State-owned Long Island Lighting Company notified the Nuclear Regulatory Commission about their evacuation plan for residents in the event of an accident at the Shoreham nuclear power plant. The plan? Area residents would be immediately evacuated to the Nassau Coliseum – unless, of course, the coliseum was being used for a hockey game, ice show or circus performance.

☞ The city council of Longmont, Colorado, apparently is hesitant to offend anyone in its jurisdiction. As proof of their unwillingness to cast a pall on anyone's day, they voted to replace all signs referring to 'dead-end streets', fearing that people might find them macabre. In their place, they would put up signs reading: NO OUTLET.

☞ How many famous Thai badminton players can you name? When you say 'badminton', do you automatically think of Thailand? Evidently, questions like this bothered Thailand's Minister of Health back in 1979. He was quite worried about the low level of badminton playing in his country. The problem, the minster finally deduced, was due to the lack of shuttlecocks. In his words: 'Time and time again, I have said that unless shuttlecocks are freely available to the people of Thailand, it will be almost impossible to increase the national badminton standard. At the present time, there are less than five hundred shuttlecocks in the country. This is the reason why the number of Thai badminton players has not matched our kingdom's population explosion.'

Readers will be glad to know that today Thailand has thousands of shuttlecocks, no doubt due to the Minister of Health, who cared enough to make badminton a priority.

☞ Three small figurines in an exhibit at Dallas City Hall happened to be nude. So the thoughtful city officials, worried that the nudity might offend some viewers, had the figurines covered with tiny handmade fig leaves.

☞ After Florida passed an 'English-only' law, counties weren't allowed to spend public funds on offering services in any foreign languages. Eager to comply to the letter, Dade County went a bit overboard: the Dade County zoo stopped including Latin names of animal species on any of its signs.

☞ Ten thousand birds were infesting a rubbish dump – and the town council was going crazy. All attempts at scaring away the birds had failed. The council finally decided to contact the Ministry of Agriculture and ask for assistance. And after six months of intensive field study, the scientists employed by the ministry camp up with the following helpful suggestions: (1) a dummy of a man should be hauled to the top of a mast and exploded – four times a day; (2) bulldozers used on the rubbish dump should be equipped with radios 'permanently tuned to classical music'; (3) council workmen should stand around the dump during the day and throw stones at the birds. A fourth recommendation that was finally cut from the scientists list proposed that 'tasty scraps soaked in hashish oil be scattered over the dump'. But the idea was scrapped because 'after a recent trial of this method, several birds fell out of the sky like bricks'.

☞ Instead of Stonehenge, why not Foamhenge? This compelling thought comes courtesy of a local government leader, who conceived it as an employment project for out-of-work labourers. Workers would recreate the stone monument in polystyrene foam, and 'the real monument could be left in its quiet glory'.

☞ In May 1994, the Islamic sect Tebrik-a-Nifaz in Pakistan announced that true Moslems should drive on the right side of the road – and sect followers did just that. The problem? Everyone else in Pakistan drives on the left side of the road. Two weeks later, the sect put out another announcement rescinding the previous one since there were so many accidents.

☞ The Wisconsin state government asked a different burning question in 1976. The state's Law Enforcement Assistance Association spent over $200,000 asking criminals to answer why they wished to escape punishment.

☞ Excessive noise from jets landing and taking off from Toledo Airport, located near Toledo, Ohio, was causing problems for residents. So, in November 1994, Toledo Mayor, Carty Finkeimer came up with a simple solution: The city should try to relocate deaf people in the high-noise area. To make this plan feasible, he suggested that the city actually help facilitate the purchase of the houses from the complainers. The idea didn't fly with the public . . . and a few days later the mayor apologised for his suggestion.

☞ In a somewhat related vein, NASA officials were apparently surprised when they couldn't find any volunteers for their latest experiment – studying the effects of blasting jet aeroplane noise into private homes for fourteen hours a day.

H

On Hand Grenades, Hard-to-Handle:

Every so often a brilliant designer comes up with a revolutionary new weapon that changes history for ever. Less often a not-too-smart designer comes up with a really stupid weapon. A weapon like Hand Grenade Number 74 (ST).

This grenade was designed by experts during World War II to blow up tanks better than regular grenades. Regular grenades are made of hard metal, and they usually bounce against enemy tanks when thrown.

The Number 74 (ST) was different, its proud designers explained. It had a special coating so it would *stick* to the enemy tanks. All the top brass and experts loved it. It was revolutionary.

In all the excitement, no one really bothered thinking about a minor question: what happened to the sticky grenade *before* it got stuck to an enemy tank?

The quick answer: it got stuck to the soldier *throwing* it. Troops using the grenade during battle found that out quickly. They usually had about five seconds to unstick themselves before the grenade that was stuck to their hands or clothes exploded.

Needless to say, there weren't many re-orders for new supplies of Hand Grenade Number 74 (ST).

On Hijacking Attempts:

In 1976, a hijacker got up from his airline seat. He took out a gun and held up a stewardess.

'Take me to Detroit,' he said.

'But we're going to Detroit already,' said the stewardess.

'Oh, good,' said the hijacker and sat back down.

On Hollywood Moguls:

A producer was pitching an idea to movie mogul Sam Goldwyn – a film adaptation of the book *The Making of Yesterday: The Diaries of Raoul de Roussy de Sales, 1938-1942*. As he kept selling the idea, pointing out why the diary would make a great film, he noticed that Goldwyn wouldn't stop staring at the book.

'How do you like that?' Goldwyn finally mused out loud. 'Four years old and the kid keeps a diary.'

On Hot Dog Storage Spots:

Sports fans are an excitable lot. So much so that, sometimes, they're so intent on the game that they just don't seem to know what they're doing.

That must have been the case with one British soccer fan, an enthusiastic supporter of the Chelsea team.

He was fined £10 for sticking a hot dog up the anus of a police horse named Eileen.

But there was good *reason* for it all. 'I was overcome with excitement after the match. I wanted to get rid of the hot dog, and just at that moment, Eileen wandered by. I intended no harm and am a genuine animal lover.'

On Honeymoons, Surprising:

Marcel Valjean and his new wife were spending a wonderful honeymoon on the lovely tropical island of Réunion in June 1977.

On the night of June 7, Valjean was returning from a midnight stroll while his wife was softly slumbering in their beautiful honeymoon cottage. As he came to the fence surrounding their tropical love nest, Valjean had an amusing idea. Why not vault over the fence into the cottage and surprise his slumbering bride?

Unfortunately, the night was dark and what Valjean thought was the fence near his honeymoon cottage was not the fence in question. Valjean instead vaulted over a fence surrounding the deadly crater of a nearby volcano – and died.

On Insecticide, Swallowing:

A Turkish farmer was taken to hospital with severe stomach pains.

After examining him, the doctor was very confused. Apparently, the farmer was suffering because he had swallowed insecticide. But there was only a very small amount in his system, which ruled out a suicide attempt. So how – or why – had the man ingested insecticide?

The farmer explained that it had been no accident. He had deliberately taken insecticide. And for good reason.

He had accidentally swallowed a fly. 'I wanted to kill it before it reproduced inside of me,' he said.

On Ideal Bible Families, Dubious:

One year the Cheshire Baptist Association decided to set up a sideshow at the Lancashire Agricultural

Fair – a tableau of mannequins showing the 'Ideal Bible Family' at home.

The problem? Where would the association get the figures they needed?

Not to worry. Help came in the form of a Madame Tussaud's Wax Museum in nearby Blackpool. The manager arranged for the fully dressed mannequins to be delivered to the fair, where the association quickly set them up and opened their doors to the public.

The whole set-up seemed perfect for the 'Let's get back to family values' theme. Viewers saw the stern but gentle father, the innocent young daughter, and the sweet loving mother sitting around a table in a humble room, looking down at the opened family Bible. And by their side, pointing at the chosen biblical passage, was the wise Baptist minister.

But most of the viewers had the nagging feeling they had seen the members of this 'Ideal Bible Family' before . . .

They were right. The association was shocked to discover that the mannequins were not your basic average God-fearing Baptists.

Instead, the wax dummy of the innocent daughter had the head and face of Snow White. The mother had the body of Queen Elizabeth and the head of a famous ice skater. The father was a well-known swindler. And as for the minister – he was the notorious murderer Dr. Crippen.

Idiotic Inventions and Products We Could Live Without

'Necessity is the mother of invention'. This old saying reveals the basic idea about inventing: as an inventor, you see a need or a problem, and then you try to invent something to fulfil that need or solve that problem. Invention's modern-day cousin, new product development, is no different.

But there are always a few inventors or product developers out there who march to a completely different drummer. They aren't going to ask themselves questions like: is it useful? Would anyone need it? Do people really *want* a combined cockroach trap and cheese grater?

No, these people boldly go forward, blithely ignoring convention, practicality, market research and basic common sense.

And so we have these brilliantly obtuse innovators to thank for this collection of utterly ridiculous inventions and products.

☞ the Tugger: originally called the Penis Uncircumcising Device (or, more casually, PUD). For the relatively small cost of $115 (plus shipping and handling), you get a custom-made device that tugs at the foreskin, slowly stretching it to cover the entire penis. After new skin is created and weights are attached (from ten to twenty-two ounces), you use this expansion device that tugs (thus the name) the penis downward by force. As *The New Republic* put it, it's 'a kind of orthodontics of the groin'.

☞ the Eight-Function Bicycle: designed by a Chinese inventor from the Dongling Machinery Plant in Shenyang. By twisting various levers, this versatile vehicle can become a tricycle, a bicycle that pedals backwards, a wheelchair, a sofa, a desk, an easel and a tripod for cameras.

☞ The Tonya Tapper: named in honour of ice skating's notorious Tonya Harding. Minneapolis lawyer David Anderson came up with the idea after hearing about the steel club Harding's henchman whacked Nancy Kerrigan with – and began marketing his own steel club by mail, for only $39.95 (plus shipping and handling). As he said in the *Minneapolis–St. Paul Star Tribune*, the Tonya Tapper might be 'the seed crystal for similar personal security products – a whole line of batons, with different colours, holsters and grips – even one of key chain size'.

☞ Dog Glasses: ever worry about Fido's eyesight? This invention, patented by a French optician in 1975, is the answer. The inventor developed them after she made sunglasses for her own dog. Just like glasses for people, they can be adjusted to different visual deficiencies – there are corrective lenses for myopic dogs; glasses for dogs recuperating from cataracts; even protective ones against wind and dust for dogs who hang their heads out of car windows.

☞ and Horse Glasses: a great bet for racehorses who just can't see straight. The patent for these was registered in 1979 and covers both corrective lenses or plain old tinted lenses, both of which also protect against dust, mud, sand and so on. The inventor claims that the optical assistance from these glasses results in better performance from the horse, because it's calmer and steadier now that it can see.

☞ a Musical Bra for Mozart Buffs: manufactured by Japanese lingerie maker Triumph International, this bra was created to honour Mozart on the two hundredth anniversary of his death. The bra contains a memory chip that plays a twenty-second selection of Mozart's music and also has lights that flash in time as the music plays. One drawback: the bra isn't washable, so it's not for everyday wear.

☞ Insecticide Pantyhose: bug-resistant pantyhose that repels spiders, cockroaches and other crawling pests. Introduced in the late 1980s by Kanebo, a Japanese textile and cosmetics company, this product actually caught on, selling over four hundred thousand pairs in the first few months. It costs only about $2 a pair.

☞ Sweet Jesus Chocolate: chocolate crucifixes with a Christ figure that bleeds red jelly when bitten into. Answering critics who claim this was in poor taste, its producer, a Canberrra, Australia, confectioner, explained that 'The object...is to put religion back into Easter with an edible icon. People who are offended by the icon have lost touch with reality. A Sweet Jesus crucifix will remind them that Easter is more than three days on the beach.'

☞ Artificial Spray-On Dirt: an enterprising West German firm came up with this clever product for all those urbanites who drive four-wheel-drive and other Jeep-type vehicles and want them to look rugged, as if they were actually used on something other than congested city streets.

☞ Freeze-Dried Pets: offered by Preserv-A-Pet. Firm owner Roger Saatzer put it succinctly: 'The next best thing to bringing [your pet] back to life is to have it freeze-dried.' With this thought in mind, his company freeze-dries dead household pets for their heartbroken owners to keep. Costs range from $450 for a basic sitting cat up to $2,000 for an attacking German shepherd.

☞ the .45 Semiautomatic Telephone: even the company that produced this telephone that looked like a gun admitted it might be a tough sell. Said Jammie Tizzard, an official of Covina, California-based S. W. Productions: 'It will be a little shocking to walk into a room and see someone holding a gun to his head, talking into it. But like any-

thing else, the public will get used to it.'
Apparently not. How many of these phones do
you see today?

☞ a One-of-a-Kind Replica of a World War I
Trench: for sale in the late 1980s by the Herbert
Hoover Presidential Library and Museum in West
Branch, Iowa. For only $7,500, you get a real-life
thirty-by-eight-foot replica of a World War I
trench, 'complete with high-tech sound and
lighting effects, robotic soldier and periscopes
with stereoscopic battlefield scenes'. An added
plus: it's wheelchair-accessible.

☞ Drive-Through Visiting Booths at Funeral
Homes: offered by Gatling's Funeral Home in
Chicago, among others. This nifty innovation
allows mourners to sign the register and view the
body live (well, sort of) on a video screen – all
without leaving the comfort of their cars. It's
great for people who have difficulty walking,
those who want to pay their respects quickly and
those who want to remain incognito for some
reason. As the owner of Gatling's put it: 'This
way the girlfriend can go through the drive-
through and pay her respects in whatever name
she chooses, while the wife is inside with the
deceased. It happens all the time.'

☞ Coffin with Escape Hatch: the perfect product
for those cautious souls who fear getting buried
alive. Newark, New Jersey, inventor Franz Vester
invented this in 1868. It's a coffin with a lid and

a tube that 'extends from the coffin up through and over the surface of the grave, said tube containing a ladder and cord, one end of said cord being placed in the hand of the person laid in the coffin, and the other end of said cord being attached to a bell on top of the square tube, so that, should a person be interred ere life is extinct, he can, on recovery to consciousness, ascend from the grave and the coffin by the ladder; or, if not able to ascend by said ladder, ring the bell, thereby giving an alarm, and thus save himself from premature burial and death'.

☞ Bird Diaper: just what it sounds like. It was designed in 1959 by Milwaukee inventor Bertha Dlugi in response to what she obviously thought was a problem: Pet birds were often allowed to fly through an owner's house, yet 'These birds cannot normally be house-trained as other pets are, and their excremental discharge is frequently deposited on household furnishings when they are at liberty, creating an unsanitary condition.' The answer to this? The bird diaper, a triangular patch of material attached to a harness that you can put around your pet parakeet or whatever.

☞ Wind Bag: a genteel name for a not-so-genteel product. The wind bag, invented in 1939, was designed 'for the receiving and storing of gas formed by the digestion of foods'. In other words, it is a fart collector. It consists of a tube with a nipple on it that you put in 'one end of the alimentary tract' (or your rectum, as the drawing with the patent application showed) and a collection chamber at the other end of the tube. It included a muffler (for obvious reasons) and a handy strap or belt that enabled you to discreetly wear the device under your clothes. Apparently (and we can't imagine why), this product never caught on.

☞ Rat Bell: another attempt by humankind to build a better mousetrap. This invention, designed in 1908, never caught on – and probably for good reason. The inventors, Joseph Barad and Edward Markoff, envisioned a fairly humane way of getting rid of mice or rats, but you have to wonder about its efficacy. The invention was a spring-resisted tripping device. When a mouse or a rat set off the trap, its head would go through a frame, where a band with a bell on it would encircle its neck. The animal is then freed – but is now wearing a collar with a bell. As the inventors explained in their application: ' "The bell-rat", as it may be termed, then in seeking its burrow or colony announces his coming by the sounds emitted by the bell, thereby frightening the other rats and causing them to flee, thus practically exterminating them in a sure and economical manner.'

☞ Tingle Pants: a stupid name for a truly stupid product. Designed for music lovers (apparently) who liked getting a real thrill as they listened to their sound systems. Tingle Pants (also called

'Rock 'n' Roll Pants') were black Lycra bikini underwear – for both men and women – with a stereo speaker in the crutch! You would wear the bikini and plug it into the output mode of your stereo and feel the vibrations in your crutch. They cost only $20, but they never really caught on, maybe because they were a little unwieldy – or maybe because no one wanted to feel the beat in their crutch.

☞ the Two Potato Clock: a clock run by potatoes...or oranges...or even beer. More specifically, this 1984 product was a digital clock that ran off the energy generated by two electrodes implanted in any acidic medium (like a potato). Time ran out quickly for this one.

☞ Pussyfoot: a cat feeder probably best-suited for people who secretly hate their cats. This product was introduced in 1979 and was an acrylic cat food dispenser that made feeding the cat a simple chore. You put food into the feeder and it would automatically dispense to the cat. Great idea for a pet owner – but not so great for the cat. The lid of the feeder had a nasty tendency to flip down while the cat was eating and hit it on the nose.

☞ the Motorised Bar Stool: a 1976 invention that's perfect for people who enjoy bellying up to the bar but who hate changing positions. With your motorised bar stool, you can zip around without ever getting up from your stool. An added plus: it has rear disc brakes.

On Juror Instructions, Suggestive:

It was a rape case in the 1970s and the victim was on the stand. As she testified, the judge noticed that one male juror was dozing. He paused and asked the victim to repeat what her attacker had said.

The victim shook her head. She was too embarrassed to repeat it. 'Okay,' the judge said, 'write down what the attacker said on a piece of paper.'

The victim did so, and this piece of paper was passed to the jury. One by one, each member took the paper, unfolded it, and read the rapist's statement, which went something like: 'Tonight I'm going to blank you like you've never been blanked before.'

Sitting next to the sleepy juror, who had gone back to dozing, was a beautiful female juror. It was her turn to read what the rapist had said. She got the paper, unfolded it, read it, then folded it again. She nudged the sleeping juror awake and handed him the paper.

He sleepily unfolded it and read the message. The

expression on his face changed into something close to absolute joy. He turned and looked at the beautiful woman. He winked at her as he stuffed the piece of paper in his pocket.

When the judge asked him for it, he blushed and shook his head. It was a personal matter, he explained.

On Journalism Students, Ones Not Bound for The New York Times:

In 1995, undergraduate journalism students at Arizona State University were given a quiz, including names that every aspiring journalist should recognise. Here are some of the answers:

- Alzheimer's: Imported beer
- Apartheid: A building in Athens
- Louis Armstrong: The first man on the moon
- Count Basie: A vampire
- Jesse Jackson: The leader of the Moral Majority.

K

On Kinky Pastimes, Animals and:

If you're thinking to try something kinky with your mate, you might be best off if you lock up your dog. Take a lesson from a couple in Fort Lauderdale, Florida.

The two decided to add some spice to their sex life by using a pair of handcuffs. One of the members of the fun couple was handcuffed to the bookcase in the bedroom. Then they both handcuffed themselves together. They were all set for a hot time when the mishap occurred.

The husband dropped the key.

He was stretching to reach it when the family dog bounded over, curious to investigate what was going on. He snuffled the floor where the key lay. The husband tried desperately to pick up the key, but it was too late.

The dog swallowed it.

And the nude couple was attached to the bookcase, with no way to unlock the handcuffs.

There they stayed, nude and extremely embarrassed,

until the police later came to free them. As they told Patrolman Fred Hansens, they were just 'fooling around' when disaster struck. 'I feel like kicking the hell out of that dog,' the man added.

On Knockouts, Unusual:

C. D. Blaylock was a heavyweight boxer at Louisiana State University in the early 1930s. Six feet tall, the boxer was noted for his unusually long reach.

One night in the ring he was facing a shorter and stockier opponent from Missouri State. In the second round, Blaylock came at his opponent with a strong right. Since it looked as if it would be a knockout if it landed, his opponent quickly tried to avoid the punch by moving closer to Blaylock. But as he did this, his head hit Baylock's right elbow.

This acted like a lever, adding even more power to Blaylock's swing. His arm completely circled the shorter man's head and wound up coming back straight at Blaylock himself. His fist crunched in his own jaw – sending him reeling against the rope. He managed to stand for a few seconds, groggily trying to stay upright. But then he collapsed and was counted out.

He had knocked himself out.

On Lectures, Odd:

Noted British journalist Auberon Waugh was accustomed to receiving lecture invitations, but this one seemed a little odd: a Senegalese magazine had invited him to go to Dakar to deliver a lecture on breast-feeding.

It seemed like an odd topic, since he ordinarily wrote and spoke on political topics. But they were offering him a free trip to Senegal – so he accepted.

He worked feverishly on his speech on this new subject. To be sure he would be understood, he even wrote his speech in French, an official language of Senegal.

He arrived in Senegal at the lecture site and began his speech. It was a 'passionate argument against the practice of breast-feeding', as he later recalled in his memoirs.

The audience of journalists, diplomats and Senegalese officials looked surprised.

It wasn't until later that he learned that the speech topic had somehow gotten garbled in the translation. It wasn't 'breast-feeding' he should have been addressing, but 'press-freedom'.

SPECIAL SECTION

Lunatic Laws:

'The law is a ass – a idiot,' says Mr. Bumble in Charles Dickens's *Oliver Twist*.

We find it hard to argue with sentiments like that, although we'd say 'an ass' and 'an idiot' like we learned in English class. In fact, almost everyone would agree that the law is an ass.

The only people who maybe wouldn't agree would be lawyers and politicians who, after all, are responsible for most laws in the first place.

So why do they make such idiotic laws? Probably because they just can't help it. Lawmakers, any psychiatrist could tell you, are almost obsessive about making laws: 'The more the merrier' seems to be their motto. And if most of the laws are absolutely idiotic, who cares?

After all, there's no law against being stupid...yet.

☞ A law added to California's books in 1953 makes it a felony for anyone to possess a blowgun. Possession of a firearm, however, is merely a misdemeanour.

☞ Federal flight regulations in Canada make no bones about it: no one, by law, can enter a Canadian aircraft while it is in flight. The law does not specify how someone could do this in the first place. In addition, no one may legally leave an aeroplane that is flying except to make a parachute jump. Those who want to make a parachute jump can't get away from the Canadian federal regulations, either. Jump from an aeroplane without a parachute in Canada and you're in major trouble – from the police. By law, anyone wanting to make a parachute jump must have a parachute or face federal prosecution.

☞ The Singapore government takes bathroom habits very seriously. In 1989, the government issued a new law levying a $510 fine for people who don't flush the toilet in public lavatories. How to enforce this law? The government cleverly enlisted a crack battalion of inspectors whose only job is to roam the public lavatories of the city and catch culprits in the act of leaving toilets unflushed.

☞ In a related measure, the Singapore government installed special sensors and cameras in lifts in most public housing apartment buildings. If any late-night carouser decides to urinate in the lift, the sensors detect this, special alarms go off, and the lift doors automatically shut until police arrive. Needless to say, Singapore has a very low crime rate – and the lowest rate of unauthorised urination in the world.

☞ A bill was introduced in Oklahoma requiring men to get advance, *written* permission from any female with whom they have sex. In addition, men would be required to tell women they could get pregnant and that pregnancy could be hazardous to health – introduced by Oklahoma State

Representative Cleta Deatherage. In a politically correct touch, she added a requirement that if a female could not read the written warnings, she must be read them in her native language. The bill was defeated.

☞ If you're packing a warhead, stay out of Chico, California. This city has a ban on nuclear weapons – with a $500 fine for anyone setting off a nuclear bomb within city limits.

☞ Texas State Representative Jim Kaster introduced a bill requiring anyone wanting to commit a crime to tell the future victim at least twenty-four hours in advance – and to notify them of the right to use deadly force.

☞ In 1980, the Wyoming legislature banned the photographing of rabbits from January through April without written permission.

☞ An anti-bigotry resolution in Walworth County, Wisconsin, in the interests of unbiased PC behaviour, took out terminology that referred to white supremacist organisations like the American Nazis as 'hate groups'. Instead, they are to be referred to as 'unhappy groups'.

☞ A British law makes it illegal for lorries to drive under bridges that are too low for them to drive under.

If you are wondering how stupid laws like the preceding can be written, we have an idea: maybe the lawyers or legislators responsible attended Bombay Law, an Indian law school that must be turning out some very unusual lawyers. Herewith, to support our hypothesis, are some questions from the LL.B. exam given at the Law School of Bombay University, India, as quoted by *The Times* of India:

☞ 'Neccesity knwows no law.' Discus.

☞ Distinguish between theft and Exfortion . . . what is defarnation?

☞ A is at work with a batchet: the bead fies off and kills a man who is standing by. Has A committed any offence?

☞ What is culpasle homicide. When does culpasle homicide amount to murder.

☞ Explain three of the exceptions to the offence of defarnation.

On Muggings, Surprising:

Mrs. Hollis Sharpe was walking her poodle, Jonathan, one night on a Los Angeles street when she was attacked by a mugger, shoved to the ground and forced to hand over her bag.

No doubt congratulating himself on his easy mugging, the mugger ran off. Unfortunately for the mugger, inside Mrs. Hollis Sharpe's bag was just one item: a plastic bag she had just finished using to scoop up after Jonathan.

On NATO Manoeuvres, Under the Weather:

In the late 1970s, NATO – the military wing of the U.S.–Western Europe alliance – was all set for White Fox. This was a military exercise to see how the alpine commandos, the elite of the NATO fighting forces, would perform under bad weather conditions.

Then the weather got foggy.

The White Fox exercise was cancelled. Why? Bad weather.

On Name Changes, Logical:

Darryl Wayne Thief was in court, charged with arson. And one of the court officers was cross-examining him, convinced that something fishy was up.

His last name wasn't actually Thief, was it? The

officer pressed the accused. Didn't Thief actually have a different last name?

The accused slowly nodded. Yes, he had given a false name, he admitted. But for a good reason. He was actually Darryl Wayne Crook, but he changed his name to Thief because Crook gave people the wrong impression.

On Nice Guys Finishing Last:

A candidate in a local election in a small town in Poland was a class-act type of guy. To show his respect and his professional courtesy for the candidate running against him, he cast his vote for his opponent.

The problem was, his was the only vote cast out of 595 eligible voters.

On Official Announcements, Afghani-Style:

According to a 1978 announcement on Afghanistan's state radio, President Noor Mohammed Taraki resigned 'due to ill health'.

They didn't elaborate on just what this ill health was – neglecting to say a word about the fact that the President just happened to have twelve bullet holes in his body.

On Obituaries, Embarrassing:

Writer Bret Harte was once working as editor of a small paper in a mining settlement in California. The wife of one of the leading citizens had died, and Harte wrote a glowing obituary. His closing line:

'She was distinguished for charity above all the other ladies of this town.'

Later on that day he went back to his office to look over the proofs for the next morning's paper. In reading over his obituary, he noticed that the compositor had made a potentially embarrassing typo. Instead of 'charity', the compositor had set 'chastity'. Harte crossed out the s, put a large query mark in the margin, and went home, relieved he had caught the error.

The next morning, he turned to the obit and was horrified. It read: 'She was distinguished for chastity (?) above all the other ladies of this town.'

On the Olympics, Ground-Breaking Events in:

The World Ploughing Association, which sponsors ploughing contests for farmers from all over the world, has applied to the Olympic Committee to sponsor ploughing contests during the Summer Olympics.

According to a disappointed association spokesperson, 'Up to now, we haven't had any reply. I, for one, can't see any real difference between ploughing and swimming.'

On Paranoia:

It was the early 1970s. The Cold War was still being waged and few Westerners had actually been behind the Iron Curtain. But in the interest of sportsmanship, the Soviet Union decided to invite a team of North American ice hockey players to play the Soviet team.

The North American team accepted, but team members were wary of what to expect behind the Iron Curtain. Their guard was up from the minute they arrived in Moscow. And when they were taken to their assigned hotel room, they became convinced that the room must be bugged. Phil Esposito, one of the hockey players, and his teammates had seen the spy movies. They knew that there had to be a microphone concealed somewhere in the room. The question was where?

Talking as normally as possible, they began carefully searching the room. No luck. The room appeared to be clean. Then one of them hit paydirt. There it was – as Esposito described it, 'a funny-looking round piece of metal on the floor, under the rug'. It had to be the bug. What else could it be?

They dug it out of the floor, proud to have out-smarted their hosts. Then came a crash from the floor beneath them.

They had unscrewed the anchor to the chandelier in the ceiling below.

On the Phone Company, Great Anal-Retentive Moments in:

A man called the phone company to get an unlisted number. He was given one and went to ask the representative on the phone about several features of phone company service. Just as he was about to hang up, he realised he had forgotten his new unlisted number. He asked the phone company representative to repeat the number to him.

'I'm sorry,' she said, 'I can't. That's an unlisted number.'

On Party Preparations:

A Houston couple were throwing a very special party for the crème de la crème of society. The two sent out invitations for, as they called it, a 'Secret Dinner' with a special guest of honour: visiting tenor Luciano Pavarotti.

They were so busy setting up their exclusive wing-ding that they didn't get around to inviting the guest of honour until the last minute. Hours before the dinner was to take place, they finally invited Pavarotti.

He said no.

On Pig Slaughtering, Stupid Innovations in:

A Romanian man had to slaughter his pig, Googo. But he was too squeamish to do this in the normal way, so instead he decided to electrocute the unlucky animal. He wired a mat of chicken wire to the local power line, figuring that the pig would eventually walk over the mat and be electrocuted. The end result would be a clean, simple, safe slaughtering job.

He and his wife waited. And finally Googo, the pig, walked over the mat. The electrical charge was so intense, the pig shot ten feet up into the air. The man ran over to see what was happening, and the pig landed on him, knocking him out. His wife ran over to revive him. In the meantime, the pig ran off and wasn't seen again.

On Politicians, Smooth:

Geoffrey Dickens, Member of Parliament, couldn't shake the attentions of one particular constituent while he was at a local fair. It was a bit irritating: here he was, pressing the flesh and mingling with his public, and this besotted, unattractive young woman continually followed him around wherever he went.

But his irritation vanished a few days later when he received a letter from her requesting a signed photograph of him. After the signature on her letter, she had written: '(Horseface)'. This touch moved him. The poor woman obviously knew her drawbacks, yet had the unassuming sense of humour to deal with them.

So he sent her the photo she requested – being sure to add the personal touch in the form of an inscription: 'To Horseface, with best wishes, Geoffrey Dickens'.

The photo was sent off and Dickens felt he had done his bit to maintain good relations with his public.

But he got a shock when his secretary later approached him and asked if he had replied to the letter. 'It was from the woman at the fair,' helpfully added the secretary. Then he added, 'I wrote "Horseface" after her name so you'd know which one she was.'

On Post Office Excuses, Bizarre:

Maybe it only happens in Great Britain. Maybe it's something about British paper, or maybe the post office boxes are oddly located ... Anyway, we submit the following for your approval, two incidents of postal service from the Twilight Zone.

One British woman, Doris Honeysett, received a ragged, torn and dirty letter in the mail. Attached to it was a brief note from the post office explaining why it was such a mess: it had been eaten by snails.

In another British postal mishap, someone wrote a letter to *The Times* complaining about the post office. The complaint? A mangled letter was returned from Windsor with the note: 'Eaten by swans'.

On the Power of Thought, Theories on:

A twenty-two-year-old Chinese man was convinced he had mastered the powers of his mind. Through his superior control of his thoughts, he believed he could cause things to happen – or not to happen.

The key, of course, was putting his theory to a test.

So he stood on a railroad track near Shanghai and applied his thoughts to a speeding train coming right at him. If his theory was correct, he could force the train to stop.

His theory was incorrect.

On Pregnancy, Bad Ways to Prevent:

In 1983, China launched an extensive twelve-month programme that was carefully designed to teach the fundamentals of birth control to the rural populace. Doctors and nurses were televised demonstrating the use of condoms and birth control pills. People were exhorted to faithfully practise the techniques.

But a scant year later the Chinese minister declared the programme a 'complete fiasco'. The birth rate had actually *increased*.

Experts were puzzled . . . until a survey was conducted. It showed that most Chinese in the hinterlands were faithfully following birth control techniques: 79 percent of the men were taking the pill every day, and 98 percent of them were carefully putting a condom on their index fingers before sex – just as demonstrated on TV.

On Plumbers,
Why Not to Amuse:

A newly married couple in Belgrade was having trouble with their sink. Unbeknownst to the wife, the husband called a plumber – who arrived at the house to work on the pipes while the wife was still out. She returned, saw a pair of legs sticking out from under the sink, and assumed it was her husband. As *The Times* of London delicately put it: 'Exactly what she did next is not certain, but it caused the plumber to bang his head into the sink above him'. His injuries were serious enough to warrant calling an ambulance. The attendants put him on a stretcher and began carrying him downstairs, when one of them asked him just what had happened.

When the plumber told him, the attendant laughed so hard he dropped the stretcher, causing the plumber to fall down the stairs and break his leg.

The plumber wound up in hospital, threatening to sue. And the wife was so upset by the entire incident that she would have nothing more to do with her husband.

On Potato Thieves, Blunders Made by:

Maybe potato thieves are dumber than the average run of thieves. Edgar Lunden was easily caught and arrested after stealing six pounds of potatoes from a supermarket. One reason for his easy apprehension? Edgar Lunden had his full name tattooed across his forehead.

But Lunden was a little surprised by his quick arrest: 'I did not think anyone would be able to identify me because I do my own tattooing, and as I used a mirror for my forehead, I got the lettering back to front.'

On Professors, Critical:

The editors of the Encyclopaedia Britannica contacted the head of a major Western university history department. They sent him a historical article that had been in the encyclopedia for years and asked him if he would be interested in revising it.

The professor promptly sent the article back with a biting note, turning down the request and commenting that the article was 'inaccurate . . . badly disorganised and full of errors'.

At this point the editors wondered who had written such a weak article. They went through their files and came up with the name – it had been written by the professor himself, many years before.

On Psychotherapy, Pressing Needs for:

Pierre Beaumard was a nervous Frenchman who just couldn't communicate well with others. He also had obsessional fears and complexes.

His therapist thought he had an answer. It was a bit unconventional, but it would work. He put Beaumard between two mattresses, and got four participants from the therapy group to walk on the mattresses, helping to 'stamp out' Beaumard's obsessions.

The cure worked. When the top mattress was removed, Beaumard had no complexes to speak of. He was dead of suffocation.

R

On Rescues, How Not to Conduct:

A man was out hunting in Arizona when he accidentally shot himself in the leg. Keeping his head about him, he realised that the best way to get help would be to alert other hunters in the area – so he fired his gun again to attract attention.

Unfortunately, he shot himself in the other leg.

On Racetrack Rescues, Death-Defying:

The Smoky Mountain Raceway ambulance happened to be a reconditioned hearse. And, as one race driver discovered, its initial use may have been a bad omen.

In 1968, during a race at the Smoky Mountain Raceway, near Maryville, Tennessee, driver Buddy Baker's car blew a tyre. The Dodge spun out of control and, at the first turn, slammed into a cement wall. Baker was alive – but badly hurt.

The raceway ambulance sped onto the track to help the injured driver. The medics got out, carefully lifted Baker onto a wheeled stretcher, loaded him into the back of the hearse, and slammed the door.

Unfortunately, the medics didn't *latch* the door.

When the driver hit the gas to quickly get away, the door flew open, and Baker zoomed onto the track, strapped to his gurney.

The speeding gurney kept moving, making its way to the straightaway. And the panicking Baker could see all the other race cars, still driving under the yellow caution flag, headed right for him.

Don Naman, the driver of the pace car that led the field, noticed Baker on the runaway gurney just ahead of him. He motioned the cars behind him to drive as close to the wall as possible, and they all watched as Baker sped past them on the stretcher, closely followed by the ambulance crew.

But it still wasn't over.

The hapless ambulance crew finally caught up to Baker and wheeled him back to the hearse, but this time he refused to go in the back – instead he rode on the front seat alongside the driver.

Bad move. From this vantage point, Baker could see just what was going on. The driver ran a red light, and another car pulled out in front of them. The hearse managed to swerve to miss the car, but it wound up on the sidewalk, where it skidded into a group of garbage cans. Finally the hearse made it to the hospital – with a flat tyre and almost no brakes.

Baker said after he was treated, the ambulance crew offered to drive him back.

'I told them, "Never mind. I'll find another ride".'

On Restaurants, Attention Grabbing:

Any self-respecting businessperson knows that image counts for a lot when it comes to attracting customers.

And Kim Chung-Hee, an enterprising South Korean businessman, was no exception. He was going to open a new restaurant/beer parlour and wanted to be sure to attract the large amount of tourists in South Korea. Since so many of the tourists were Europeans, specifically Germans, he thought long and hard about what would grab their attention. He specifically wanted a name with 'an authentic European ring', as he put it.

It wasn't easy. Kim described himself as no student of history. But finally he came up with the perfect attention-grabbing name.

The Hitler.

He even bought a number of swastika flags to hang on the walls, 'Korea guarantees liberty of expression to its people', he said.

Shortly after his restaurant opened, however, the Mayor of Seoul asked him to change the name to 'something less controversial'.

On Rescues by the Military, Great Moments in:

During a firemen's strike in 1978, the British Army took over the normal duties of firemen. And typically, one cold January day, they were called by a little old lady to rescue her cat, stuck high in a tree. The Army accomplished its mission quickly and efficiently. The cat came down and the thankful little old lady invited the soldiers in for tea.

Afterward, full of tea and biscuits, the soldiers waved good-bye – and ran over the cat.

On Radio, Confusing Moments in:

King George VI and his wife Queen Elizabeth were making a trip across Canada in 1939. Wherever they went, radio broadcasters followed their every move.

In Winnipeg, the royal couple was greeted by the Canadian Prime Minister, MacKenzie King. They were also greeted by the mayor of Winnipeg and his wife – Mr. and Mrs. Queen.

The Canadian Broadcasting Corporation announcer had his work cut out for him doing a coherent on-the-spot report: 'Here comes the royal family now. The automobile has now stopped, a member of the RCMP is opening the car door – oh, there's the King – he's stepping out, followed by Her Majesty Queen Elizabeth, nattily attired in a silver coat. Mr. King is now shaking hands with the King and introducing Mr. Queen to the King and Queen and then Mrs. Queen to the Queen and King. They are now proceeding up the steps to the well-decorated City Hall, the King and Mr. King together, with the Queen being escorted by Mrs. Queen. The King has now stopped and said something to Mrs. Queen and goes to Mrs. Queen and the Queen and Mr. King and the Queen laughed jovially. The King leaves Mr. King and goes to Mrs. Queen and the Queen and Mr. King follow behind . . . .'

SPECIAL SECTION
Science Goes Stupid:

Einstein working through abstruse mathematical formulas to arrive at relativity, Watson and Crick painstakingly figuring out the helical structure of DNA, Max Planck elucidating the uncertainty of the universe with his formulation of quantum mechanics...

From our perspective, so what?

Yes, these were great moments of human achievement, but did they make anyone laugh?

In compiling this section, we avoided like the plague the great triumphs by the greatest minds in history.

We were on the lookout for littler minds. If you look at life like a great television schedule in the sky, we were on the lookout for cheap sitcom reruns.

We wanted the kind of science that swallows grant money or taxpayers' money and, at the end of it all, doesn't advance humankind one bit – or maybe even regresses us all a notch or two.

But this kind of science gets a laugh or two. And if you're a hardworking taxpayer, maybe you too can laugh when you realise where some of your hard-earned money is going.

☞ In 1990, researchers at the University of Wisconsin–Madison embarked on a scientific study of rhinotillexomania – better known as nose-picking. They sent out questionnaires to twelve hundred people – containing such deep questions as 'What finger do you use when picking your nose?' and 'After picking your nose, how often do you find yourself looking at what you have removed?'

☞ One professor decided to turn his research into a moneymaking enterprise. Dr. Terence Glanville studied wood lice at the University of Nottingham – and came up with a great idea: wood lice racing. He designed a ten-lane wood lice track upon which lice with numbers painted on their backs could race. To make it even more exciting, people could cover the course with a damp cloth, which increased the speed of the lice. Back in 1984, Glanville was convinced he was onto something huge. 'I am convinced wood lice racing will take off in a big way.' We're still waiting.

☞ A British governmental committee needed a definitive ruling on when winter begins and when it ends – so they turned to the Meteorological Office in Bracknell. The scientific reply: 'Winter begins when all the leaves have fallen off the trees. And it ends when the bulbs start coming up again.'

☞ In late 1994, Utah State University got a whopping $500,000 research grant from the Environmental Protection Agency – to study bovine flatulence. The researchers will round up rangeland cattle and fit them with special breathing devices – to measure just how much methane cows release when they burp. This isn't the only study of this kind. In fact, this Utah State study will expand on a previous bovine flatulence study (a mere $300,000 one) begun in 1991 by Washington State University, which, to quote an Associated Press story, 'provoked widespread ridicule'.

☞ Psychobiologist Harman Peeke of the University of California at San Francisco ran a $102,000 research study funded by taxpayers' dollars to answer the burning question: are sunfish that drink tequila more aggressive than sunfish that drink gin? (For his efforts, he won Senator William Proxmire's Golden Fleece award for wasting taxpayers' dollars – which cost him his federal grant and forced him to drop his project.)

☞ Another Golden Fleece award went to the National Institute of Mental Health for funding a $97,000 study of ethnicity in the highlands of Peru. The anthropologists were researching relationships between Indians and mestizos (mixed-blood Indians) in the Peruvian Andes – and as part of their research, investigated a Peruvian brothel to, as the research article put it, 'obtain a good idea of its everyday functioning'. One researcher, Dr. Pierre L. van der Berghe of the University of Washington, defended himself by saying it was only one aspect of the study. Moreover, he said, it was his research associate Dr. George Primov's idea to write about the brothel. Furthermore, it only cost about $50 and it was 'something he did mostly in the evenings'.

☞ A study at the Royal University of Stockholm, Sweden, found that old people move their legs with greater speed when they are in a hurry.

☞ Most people eat lunch because they are hungry. This finding was 'revealed' from a study done by Taiwan's Council for Agricultural Planning and Development. The study also found that other people ate lunch because they like to eat three meals a day, and lunch was one of the three meals.

☞ An earth-shattering study by Dr. Norris Thomson has found that people who don't go to the doctor much don't go because they aren't sick.

☞ Reverse Speech Technology has been involved in research probing 'reverse speech'. More precisely, this group holds that when you play recorded speech backwards you can discover unconscious 'reverse' messages that the speakers are masking – not 'Paul is dead', but such insightful words as these uncovered by playing back CNN reporter John Holliman during his Gulf War coverage.

His on-air statement: 'The anti-aircraft fire is now going to the south. We're looking out to the west and we see the tracer bullets going.'

This played backwards, revealed the following hidden message: 'To hell with it. The bastards don't know it's Fonzie. Don't tell them it's yesterday.'

On Spies, Crackerjack:

It was 1975 and the Basque separatist movement in Spain had everyone on tenterhooks. There had been terrorist bombings, threats of further violence and the like.

In the midst of this tension, two undercover agents from the Civil Guard were on duty in Vitoria. They noticed three suspicious-looking men and began covertly following them from the evening well into the night. When the three suspects entered a Basque nightclub at midnight, the undercover agents were more convinced than ever that their hunch was right and followed them in. It was time to trap their prey.

They saw the men sitting in a corner, but when they marched over, prepared to arrest them, the three men turned the tables. They jumped up, grabbed the unsuspecting agents, pulled the agents' arms behind their backs, and pushed them out of the building.

The three 'terrorists' explained that they were undercover agents, working for the Civil Guard, who had been tailing the other two men – because they looked suspicious.

On Safety Demonstrations:

William Michini was an ex-Philadelphia fireman with a point to prove. He had been fired for having long hair – which the fire department claimed was a safety threat.

Michini decided not to take his dismissal sitting down. Instead, he took his case to federal court.

In court, he argued that his hair didn't interfere with his duties. It wasn't unsafe at all. In fact, he claimed, hair couldn't burn. It was self-extinguishing. To demonstrate his claim, he confidently struck a match and held it to his head.

He set his head on fire.

On Shark Attacks, Why Your Public Relations Expert Knows Best:

Beachgoers at the town of South Padre Island, Texas were beginning to go into a panic. Everyone was whispering about it: 'Sharks! Don't go in the water!' The word was spreading that two women had been bitten by sharks while swimming at the beach.

Not to worry, said town spokesman Joe Rubio. It wasn't a shark attack, but a shark *accident*. 'More than likely he ran into her leg and got it caught in his mouth.'

On Separation Celebrations, Bang-Up:

Cesar de Mana, a Brazilian fisherman, was a happy man. After some not-so-blissful wedded years, his wife had finally agreed to a separation. So the newly freed Mana invited three women over for a festive dinner – which he would cook himself. It was time for a real bang-up celebration – and that's just what de Mana got.

The wine flowed and de Mana and friends became cheerfully drunk... and hungry. So the slightly sodden de Mana went into the kitchen to cook his speciality – sausages. He grabbed four of them, tossed them in the pan, and began frying.

A split second later, the kitchen – in fact, the entire house – blew up. He and his guests wound up the celebration by staying in the hospital.

He had thrown four sticks of dynamite into the frying pan by mistake.

On Small Talk,
Disastrous:

An English aristocrat was sitting in a box next to
Lord North and started a conversation with him.
He noticed two women walk into the box directly
opposite and chose it as a topic of conversation.

'Who is that ugly woman who just came in?'

Lord North smiled. 'Oh, that is my wife,' he said
pointedly.

His companion grew flustered. 'Sir, I beg your
pardon. I do not mean her. I mean that shocking
monster who is along with her.'

'That,' replied Lord North, 'is my daughter.'

On Stock Market Moves,
Stupid:

The grandfather of 1940s' movie star Lana Turner
was an early major investor in a struggling soft drink
company called Coca-Cola.

The drink tasted good enough, the grandfather
reasoned. But he wasn't completely sure about his
investment. He became convinced that that awful
name was going to kill sales.

He sold out and put the money into a more promising corporation, one that had a product which he knew would take the world by storm: the Raspberry Cola Company.

On Stupid Ways of Pretending You Know Who You're Talking to:

Mrs. Richard Harding Davis, a socially prominent woman, was travelling on the Long Island Rail Road when another woman approached her. It was wonderful to see her again, the woman said. It had been too long!

During the niceties, Mrs. Davis desperately tried to remember who this stranger was. The face was familiar, but she drew a blank when it came to the woman's name.

Oblivious to the fact that the Mrs. Davis didn't remember her, the second woman went on talking. Then Mrs. Davis thought she might have found a way out of the predicament, when her unknown companion mentioned her brother.

'Your brother,' Mrs. Davis said eagerly. 'Of course, I couldn't forget your brother. And what is he doing now?'

Her companion looked at her oddly. 'My brother,' she – Mrs. Douglas Robinson, sister of Teddy Roosevelt – said, 'is still President of the United States.'

On Scottish Mountain-Climbing Feats:

Mr. Kenneth Campbell of Sutherland, Scotland had a dream. To ascend to the peak of Ben Nevis dragging a 250-pound organ.

His first noble attempt failed, probably due to the wrong choice of instrument. He was pushing a grand piano up Ben Nevis when the piano crashed over a low cliff and dragged Campbell a hundred feet after it

Undaunted, Campbell returned home, hitched himself to an organ, and vowed to try again. He started immediately. His routine was simple. He would pull the organ a mile or two, then set up camp at night. Each morning after awakening, he would eat some porridge, then play a resounding chorus of 'These Are My Mountains' and set on his way. The *Glasgow Herald* in 1971 reported him well above the snowline, organ in hand.

It was all for a good cause. 'I'm doing it all to aid cancer research,' Campbell said.

◆ＳＰＥＣＩＡＬ　ＳＥＣＴＩＯＮ◆

Stupid Songs:

You can divide all music, like Caesar did Gaul, into three basic types.

There are the few great pieces. In this case, we don't necessarily mean just the classics, we mean any type that you can't get out of your head, the type that somehow makes you cry every time.

Then there's the great majority. The so-so stuff. You don't love it, you don't hate it. You listen. And you forget.

And there's the rare few, the precious few, that are beautifully, unbelievably stupid. Unfortunately, this book isn't multimedia, so we could include the awful music itself. But the stupid lyrics and song titles included here speak for themselves. So, without further ado, here's our collection of stupid songs, a hit parade of hysteria.

☞ One of the first feminist pop songs was the multicultural 'Wigwam Bam'. According to a write-up about it in *Record Mirror*, it told the 'consciousness-raising tale of how squaw Mini Ha Ha shed her culturally determined position of subservience and took on the dominant role of predator with the joyous yell: 'Wigwam bam/ gonna make you my man!'

☞ Kudos for the longest stupid song title goes to this song, written in 1941: 'I'm Looking for a

Guy Who Plays Alto and Baritone and Doubles on a Clarinet and Wears a Size Thirty-Seven Suit'. It was a hit.

☞ Stacey Hart, the 'Saucy Songstress', won National Condom Week's competition for her catchy song – a comedy rap number called 'Jiggy, Jiggy, Jiggy – Slip It On!'

☞ 'I'm Vasectomised' reached number three on the Thai charts in the early 1980s.

☞ 'The Drunk Driver' by Ferlin Husky is a cautionary country ditty that leaves you weeping. To put it as simply as possible, it's about a husband who, after an intense argument with his wife, goes to drown his sorrows at a nearby bar. When he later drunkenly drives home, he accidentally puts his car into reverse and runs over his own children.

☞ Points for great song name and lyrics have to go to the not-memorable song sung by British singer Melodie Suggs: 'You Dun Stomped on My Heart'. Wails Suggs, 'You dun stomped on my heart/you dun mashed that sucker flat. You dun sorta/stomped on my aorta...'

☞ A 1979 Italian disco chart-topper about Pope John Paul II included the catchy lyrics: 'He's the groove, he's the man, that new Pope in the Vatican....'

T

On Theme Restaurants, Stupid Moments in:

. It wasn't the most appetising idea for a restaurant, but Gordon and Jasmine Geisbrecht thought they had a real winner.

In the mid-70s, they opened a restaurant in Winnipeg, Manitoba called The Outhouse.

They carried the entire bathroom theme into the interior design. Toilet bowls alternated with tables in the main dining room, and a toilet seat appeared as a logo on all the menus. But the restaurant wasn't a success – chiefly because it was forced to close shortly after opening.

The problem? Not enough *working* bathrooms.

On Thieves, Not-So-Smart:

In Vang, Norway a group of professional thieves were carrying out a carefully planned robbery. Everything was going like clockwork.

They broke into a company at night, located the safe and set up an explosive charge that would just blow the door of the safe off, enabling them to get to the money inside. After setting the fuse, they ran into the next room, crouched behind the wall and waited for the explosion.

It came a few seconds later. The safe door was blown off. So was the roof. In fact, the entire building collapsed, trapping the robbers, still crouching in the next office, under the rubble.

There had been one problem they hadn't foreseen: instead of money, the safe had been filled with dynamite.

On Train Stations, Stupid:

Passengers waiting for the train at a station in Hampshire saw their train pull in – but instead of letting them on, they heard an announcement.

'You are not to board this train which has only stopped to let you know that it does not stop here on Sundays.'

Unbelievably, the train then pulled out. A British Rail spokesman explained that this was an 'economy measure' to save power. Passengers walked to the next station, where they were let on.

On Tourist, Confused:

Mr. Nicholas Scotti was happy, sitting on the airplane. He was going back to his native country of Italy after years of living in San Francisco.

En route to Italy, the plane made a refuelling stop at New York's Kennedy Airport. Mr. Scotti, who didn't speak English too well, misunderstood the words 'refuelling stop'. Thinking he had arrived at his destination, he got off the plane and went into the airport.

His nephews weren't there to meet him, but Mr. Scotti assumed they had been caught in the notorious Roman traffic they had told him about in their letters. So he found his own way out of the airport.

He *was* a little surprised at the great number of changes that had occurred in Italy since he had left – but, after all, this was 1977 and it was natural to assume that many old monuments had been destroyed. It was also somewhat surprising to find how many people spoke English, but, after all, American tourists were everywhere. Why, the government had even put up street signs in English for their benefit!

But Mr. Scotti didn't have time for speculation. He had some relatives to meet. So he asked a passing police officer in Italian for directions to the bus terminal. The policeman, who by the best of coincidences happened to be from Naples, answered in fluent Italian, and Mr. Scotti followed his directions and found the bus terminal, where he boarded a bus. After many fruitless attempts to understand Mr. Scotti and to help the man find his nephews, the bus driver turned him over to another policeman, who this time didn't speak Italian. This prompted Mr. Scotti to complain out loud about the absurdity of the Italian government, employing policemen who couldn't speak the language.

Finally the mystery was solved – but not for Mr. Scotti. Even when told (in Italian) that he was in the wrong city and the wrong country, Mr. Scotti refused to believe he had been in error. As a police escort sped him back to Kennedy Airport, he pointed at the speeding cars outside the car window and said, 'See? I know I'm in Italy. That's how they drive.'

On Timetables, Useful:

Passengers in Staffordshire were angry.

The buses on the route from Hanley to Bagnall weren't stopping at bus stops to pick them up.

A bus company official heard their complaints. Yes, it was true, he said. But he had a clear explanation.

If the buses stopped, the timetable wouldn't be accurate.

On Tourists, Overly Compliant:

It was a damp November in 1979, and a group of tourists were sightseeing in the Palace of Westminster.

The Lord Chancellor, Lord Hailsham, was walking across the lobby of the House of Commons, when he spotted his friend, Member of Parliament Neil Marten. Remembering that it was Marten's birthday, Hailsham waved to his friend and yelled out, 'Neil!'

At that command, the entire group of tourists immediately fell to their knees in prayer.

On Train Companies, Stupid Routine Excuses by, Part 1:

In another great moment from British Rail, Professor Sir Roland Smith complained about fleas in a sleeping car. He got a 'personal' letter of apology from the chief of British Rail, Sir Bob Reid, along with an attached memo that said: 'Send standard flea letter'.

On Train Companies, Stupid Routine Excuses by, Part 2:

In yet another great moment, a spokesman for British Rail explained the company's ultimate non-discrimination attitude: 'Would-be saboteurs have a perfect right to be on the platform, provided they have bought a ticket. It is not the job of our staff to arrest passengers carrying rocket-launchers . . .'

On Translations, Enthusiasm for:

When governor of California, Ronald Reagan delivered a speech in Mexico City; he didn't speak Spanish, so he made his speech in English. Nevertheless, he was a bit disappointed by the tepid applause he received and more than a bit embarrassed – especially when the speaker who followed him, who was speaking in Spanish, was greeted with enthusiastic applause after each paragraph. To hide his embarrassment, Reagan joined in with the enthusiastic applause and, in fact, did the audience one better. He began clapping before anyone else did and continued clapping after everyone else stopped.

Then the U.S. ambassador leaned over. 'I wouldn't do that if I were you,' he said to the governor. 'He's interpreting your speech.'

On Terrorist Groups, Not-So-Terrifying:

The Gatti Gang was Italy's answer to Joey Gallo's Gang That Couldn't Shoot Straight. The Milan-based cell of the notorious Red Brigade, this gang wasn't as much notorious for its terrorist activities as for its inspired bungling.

Being a terrorist gang requires a number of basic elements. You have to plan terrorist acts, you have to raise the money and then gather the weapons to commit these acts; and you have to commit them. The Gattis typically failed on all three fronts.

First of all, the gang often couldn't hold their important strategy sessions, because Enrico Gatti, their leader, suffered from debilitating colds. When they did manage to strategise, they faced another roadblock: When you're a member of a subversive group, you often have to raise money by illegal methods – like robberies. Problem was, none of the twenty-eight Gatti Gang members could drive a car.

But what they lacked in driving ability, they made up for in determination. They took buses everywhere, robbed one bank using a getaway motor scooter, and generally kept plugging. And they were successful . . . marginally. An example of one of their better hauls: 18,000 lira or about $10.

Most terrorist groups also have a decent amount of weapons. But not the Gattis. They had only one bomb for the years when they were theoretically terrorising the countryside – and they were too scared of the bomb to actually use it. (This prompted another terrorist to tell them to toss in the towel because they were a danger to everyone.)

Their guns were so old that they couldn't be fired – so the Gattis tried to replace them, but were taken for $2,000 when the arms deal blew up.

The Gatti Gang went out with as much of an idiotic flair as they conducted business. After ten years, Enrico Gatti finally had enough and gave himself up. He gave an impassioned speech in the courtroom and eloquently urged his followers: 'Desert! It's all over. Ten years of struggle have brought us nothing but tears. Lots of our young members want to go home and live in peace.'

On Vacuum Cleaner History, Decisive Moments in:

The inventor of the vacuum cleaner was a British gentleman named Hubert Cecil Booth. The almost-inventor of the vacuum cleaner was a brilliantly stupid American inventor who gave his idea to Booth.

What happened was this. Booth was visiting a London music hall in 1901 when he saw that one of the acts was an American who was demonstrating his carpet-dust-removing machine.

The machine was a box with a bag on top. It worked . . . sort of. The problem was that it *blew* the dust off the carpet. After the show, Booth went to the inventor. 'It should suck, not blow,' he said.

The American was furious. 'Suck? Suck? Sucking is not possible,' he said as he stormed past Booth.

On Weathermen:

In April of 1994, the newscaster on the main evening news show in New Delhi, India made a startling announcement: 'The weather has been cancelled until further notice. It's all got too complicated to explain and we keep getting it wrong anyway.'

It was a logical move, given the trouble the news station had been having.

Said a spokesman for the station in *The Times* of India the following Sunday: 'It's been an abnormal April with, quite literally, scorching sunshine one minute and bitter winds and rain the next. On Monday evening, our weatherman told viewers, quite literally, to keep their woollen underwear on, and next day the temperature was 102. On Tuesday, he promised more sunshine, and we had four inches of snow. He's a professional meteorologist, and, when the death threats from viewers came in, he took it all very personally. He spent all Wednesday quite literally memorising a long report, and tried to explain the freak conditions using satellite pictures, but, halfway through the evening broadcast, he forgot what he was talking about, and, quite literally, he couldn't go on. He just kept smiling nervously and adjusting his tie while repeating, 'If the snow cover over the Himalayas is sparse, it will surely lead to a good monsoon,' until he started to cry and eventually we quite literally faded him out.

'We haven't seen him since. We'll try him again next month, though. It's always blazing hot every day in May, so he should be able to cope. But I'm not sure he will return. His granny was attacked by an irate farmer with a chainsaw. Quite literally.'

On Yellow Streetlights, Little-Known Facts About:

The Bedford Gas and Light Company in 1979 announced plans to put in yellow streetlights at a town on Cape Cod.

But Lois Crane, a colour consultant, launched an angry campaign against them. The reason? Yellow, combined with the red traffic lights, would incite people to have wild sex.

But people were not convinced. What about some proof, some scientific *evidence* for this theory?

Crane was not deterred. She had proof.

'I once drove past a motel with amber lights in Washington. I wanted to scream, throw rocks, dance naked and copulate – all at the same time. But I managed to restrain myself because I am seventy-three.'